A People's History of the Russian Revolution

Join the Left Book Club

Membership of the Left Book Club costs just £40 a year, for which you will receive four specially commissioned or licensed titles each year, plus other members' benefits, such as access to events, newsletters, and special offers on non-LBC titles.

To join please visit www.leftbookclub.com

Also available

Here We Stand
Women Changing the World
Helena Earnshaw and
Angharad Penrhyn Jones

Being Red
A Politics for the Future
Ken Livingstone

Syriza
Inside the Labyrinth
Kevin Ovenden
Foreword by Paul Mason

Sound System
The Political Power of Music
Dave Randall

Cut Out
Living Without Welfare
Jeremy Seabrook

The Rent Trap
How We Fell Into It and
How We Get Out of It
Rosie Walker and Samir Jeraj

A People's History of
the Russian Revolution

Neil Faulkner

PlutoPress
www.plutobooks.com

First published 2017 by Pluto Press
345 Archway Road, London N6 5AA

www.plutobooks.com

Copyright © Neil Faulkner 2017

The right of Neil Faulkner to be identified as the author of this work
has been asserted by him in accordance with the Copyright, Designs
and Patents Act 1988.

The Left Book Club, founded in 2014, company number 9338285 pays
homage to the original Left Book Club founded by Victor Gollancz in 1936.

British Library Cataloguing in Publication Data
A catalogue record for this book is available from the British Library

ISBN   978 0 7453 9904 1   Hardback
ISBN   978 0 7453 9903 4   Paperback
ISBN   978 1 7868 0019 0   PDF eBook
ISBN   978 1 7868 0021 3   Kindle eBook
ISBN   978 1 7868 0020 6   EPUB eBook

This book is printed on paper suitable for recycling and made from fully
managed and sustained forest sources. Logging, pulping and manufacturing
processes are expected to conform to the environmental standards of the
country of origin.

Typeset by Stanford DTP Services, Northampton, England

Simultaneously printed in the United Kingdom and United States of America

Contents

Series Preface

The first Left Book Club (1936–48) had 57,000 members, had distributed 2 million books, and had formed 1,200 workplace and local groups by the time it peaked in 1939. LBC members were active throughout the labour and radical movement at the time, and the Club became an educational mass movement, remodelling British public opinion and contributing substantially to the Labour landslide of 1945 and the construction of the welfare state.

Publisher Victor Gollancz, the driving force, saw the LBC as a movement against poverty, fascism, and the growing threat of war. He aimed to resist the tide of austerity and appeasement, and to present radical ideas for progressive social change in the interests of working people. The Club was about enlightenment, empowerment, and collective organisation.

The world today faces a crisis on the scale of the 1930s. Capitalism is trapped in a long-term crisis. Financialisation and austerity are shrinking demand, deepening the depression, and widening social inequalities. The social fabric is being torn apart. International relations are increasingly tense and militarised. War threatens on several fronts, while fascist and racist organisations are gaining ground across much of Europe. Global warming threatens the planet and the whole of humanity with climate catastrophe. Workplace organisation has been weakened, and social democratic parties have been hollowed out by acceptance of pro-market dogma. Society has become more atomised, and mainstream politics suffers an acute democratic deficit.

Yet the last decade has seen historically unprecedented levels of participation in street protest, implying a mass audience for progressive alternatives. But socialist ideas are no longer, as in the immediate post-war period, 'in the tea'. One of neoliberalism's achievements has been to undermine ideas of solidarity, collective provision, and public service.

The Left Book Club aspires to meet this ideological challenge. Our aim is to offer high-quality books at affordable prices that are carefully selected to address the central issues of the day and to be accessible to a wide general audience. Our list represents the full range of progressive traditions, perspectives, and ideas. We hope the books will be used as the basis of reading circles, discussion groups, and other educational and cultural activities relevant to developing, sharing, and disseminating ideas for change in the interests of the common people at home and abroad.

The Left Book Club collective

Acknowledgements

My understanding of the Russian Revolution has been shaped by countless lectures, meetings, and discussions involving hundreds of revolutionary activists. It is impossible to recall, let alone list, all those who, at different times and in different ways, have influenced my perspective.

I should perhaps record that, from 1980 to 2010, I was an active member of the Socialist Workers Party in Britain. For much of that time, especially in the 1980s, I believe the SWP to have been a small but effective revolutionary organisation that punched above its weight. I also believe it to have been a powerhouse of Marxist theory. Its degeneration into a self-referencing and self-perpetuating sect is, in my view, a tragic development in the history of the British Left.

But it would be dishonest not to make it clear that most of what I know about revolution – both as historian and activist – I owe to the SWP of the 1980s. I therefore owe a deep debt of gratitude to all the SWP comrades alongside whom I fought the Nazis, supported the miners, refused to pay the poll tax, and, when we had time, debated the history of the international working-class movement.

Since 2010, I have formed many new and rewarding political friendships, and these have contributed, I believe, to a richer, more nuanced understanding of the Russian Revolution. Not least, the degeneration of the British Left over the last two or three decades – which is a generic process, not something restricted to the SWP – has given me a clearer understanding that revolutionary parties are built by the masses themselves in struggle; that is, they do not arise from voluntarism, from acts of will by self-appointed revolutionary 'vanguards'; they do not arise from what has sometimes been called 'the primitive accumulation of cadre'. Revolutionaries should organise. But they should never proclaim themselves to be *the* party. Only the masses in struggle can create a party of revolution.

I should give special thanks to two of those new friends, David Castle of Pluto Press and Nik Gorecki of Housmans Bookshop and the Left Book Club, for critical comments on the first draft of this book. The final version is, in consequence, much improved.

Dates, Names, Prices, and Wages

Russia used the Julian Calendar until 1918. This was 13 days behind the Gregorian Calendar. Thus, for example, the Storming of the Winter Palace took place on 25/26 October according to the Julian Calendar, but 7/8 November according to the Gregorian. I have used Julian dates for events in Russia before the adoption of the Gregorian system.

The transliteration of Russian names into English is inconsistent. In each case, I have tried to choose a convenient form and stick to it. A further problem arises from changes in name, of which there have been many, due to war and revolution, in the last century of Russian history. St Petersburg is an obvious example: it has been St Petersburg (before the First World War), Petrograd (1914–24), Leningrad (1924–91), and is now St Petersburg again.

There are occasional references to prices, so it is worth knowing that one rouble was equal to about 50 US cents, and there were 100 kopeks to a rouble, so one kopek was worth about half a cent. A loaf of black bread cost about 40 kopeks in 1914, but more than three times as much in 1917. Wartime inflation averaged about 500 per cent across the full range of consumer necessities. Wages increased at barely half this rate, from perhaps two roubles a day for a skilled worker to four or five; low-paid workers might receive as little as the price of a loaf. It is safe to assume that living standards, already pitifully low, plummeted during the war.

Map 1   The Russian Empire in 1917

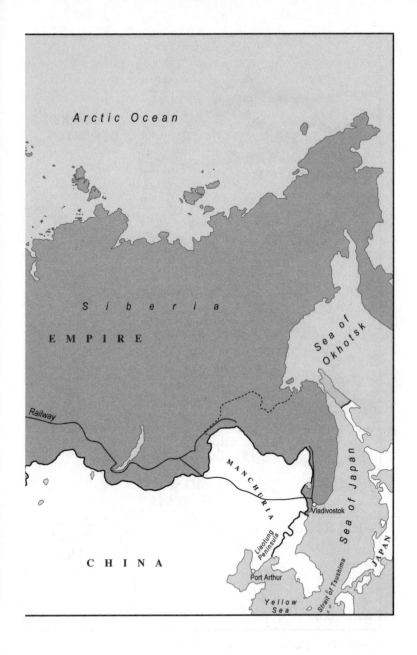

Map 2 Petrograd during the Revolution

1 Russky Renault Factory
2 New Lessner Factory
3 Moskovsky Regiment Barracks
4 Sukhanov's Apartment
5 First Machine Gun Regiment Barracks
6 Erikson Factory
7 Schlusselburg Fortress
8 Finland Station
9 Kshesinskaya Mansion
10 Peter and Paul Fortress
11 Trinity Bridge
12 Alexandrovsky Bridge
13 Taurida Palace
14 Smolny Institute
15 Palace Square
16 Winter Palace
17 Pavlovsky Guard Barracks
18 Liteiny Prospect
19 Lithuanian Guard Barracks
20 Preobrazhensky Guard Barracks
21 Volynsky Guard Barracks
22 Finland Guard Barracks
23 Cruiser 'Aurora'
24 Nikolaevsky Bridge
25 Central Telegraph Office
26 Central Post Office
27 Keksgolmsky Regiment Barracks
28 War Ministry
29 Admiralty
30 St Isaac's Cathedral
31 Marinsky Palace
32 Petrograd Telephone Station
33 Kazan Cathedral
34 State Bank
35 City Duma
36 Alexandrinsky Theatre
37 Znamenskaya Square
38 Semenovsky Guard Barracks
39 Kronstadt Naval Base
40 Ismailovsky Guard Barracks
41 Warsaw Station
42 Putilov Factory
43 Tsarskoe Selo Palace

Introduction

The Russian Revolution is probably the most misunderstood event in world history. This book aims to mark the centenary of the revolution by setting the record straight. It is an attempt to describe a lived experience of mass democracy and popular revolt that 'shook the world'; an attempt to show that it was the collective action of millions of ordinary men and women that powered the historical process between 1917 and 1921; and an attempt to show a new generation of people eager for change that another world is indeed possible, and that it all depends on what we, all of us, rising from our slumber, choose to do.

In essence, the Russian Revolution was an explosion of democracy and activity from below. It transformed the millions of people who took part in it, and inspired tens of millions who watched. It shook the world capitalist system to its foundations and came close to bringing it down. It offered a tantalising glimpse of a radically different world – a world without bosses and police, a world of democracy, equality, and peace.

But, sadly, only a glimpse. In the end, the forces defending the system – the millionaires, the statesmen, the generals, the churches, the tabloid press, the fascist squads, the fake 'socialists' in red ties, the 'sell-out' union bureaucrats – these forces, across most of Europe, proved too powerful. The revolutionary tide receded. The Russian Revolution was left isolated and besieged. And eventually – impoverished, devastated by war, threatened with invasion – it fell to pieces and was consumed by the most murderous counter-revolutionary terror in history.

This book sets out to nail three bogus arguments about the Russian Revolution – arguments we are likely to hear repeated many times this centenary year. It aims to show that:

- Lenin was a democrat, not a 'democratic centralist', and that the Bolshevik Party was a mass democratic movement, not a pseudo-revolutionary sect.
- The revolution was a mass movement of the people based on participatory democracy, not a coup to set up a dictatorship.
- Stalinism was a counter-revolutionary movement that destroyed the Bolshevik Party and Soviet democracy.

This does not mean that the book is original. This is an odd thing for an author to admit, since we mostly want to claim 'originality' for our work. Why read it otherwise? Let me explain.

Readers who like this book – especially readers interested in the lessons for present-day activism – should immediately consider reading Trotsky's *History of the Russian Revolution*. It is very long, but it is written with such style and panache, the story it tells is of such drama and significance, and the author, a leading participant as well as the revolution's supreme historian, was gifted with an intellect of such astonishing interpretive power, that you are likely to find it one of the most important books you ever read. It is not simply the greatest narrative of one of history's most earth-shaking events; it is, quite simply, a complete manual of revolutionary strategy and tactics.

I cannot claim originality because Trotsky has been my guide throughout. I have, of course, read much else. Some of this wider reading I have drawn upon and referenced. But much I have not. This is because much of it is poor fare. The reason is political. Until the end of the Cold War, Western scholarship was dominated by a caricature of the Bolshevik Revolution which saw it as a 'Leninist' coup to install a dictatorship, while Eastern scholarship provided a distorted image of this caricature by proclaiming the monstrous Stalinist dictatorship of the 1930s to be a lineal descendant of the workers' state of 1917–21.

Since the Eastern European revolutions of 1989 and the fall of the Berlin Wall, archives have opened and scholarship has become more relaxed. Much good, honest, fresh research has been done. But this has either amplified aspects of the interpretation offered here, or, following the principle 'better informed but none the wiser', has been deployed in the service of the dreary conspiracy theories of the Cold War past.

Here, on the other hand, we celebrate the creative power of the common people when they organise together and rise in struggle against their oppressors. For revolution is essentially a concentrated expression – concentrated in time and space – of the common people's age-old yearning for freedom, justice, and decency. It is a moment when the drip-drip of partial reform in normal times – always too little, too late – accelerates into a sudden cascade of change, a torrent of transformation, that 'shakes the world' and threatens to 'turn it upside down'.

This is a book about the past for the present. It is not a book for academics who merely study the world, but one for activists who want to change it. And we must change it, for, a century on, the world capitalist system that the Bolsheviks attempted to destroy now constitutes an existential threat, a clear and present danger, to the well-being, even survival, of humanity and the planet.

So the book is weighted heavily towards the lead-up to the revolution as opposed to its aftermath. That reflects our place in history, standing before the revolution we need to make, not after it. The immediate questions we face concern how you make a revolution, not what you do during one, let alone how you remake the world after one.

I find a lot of contemporary discussion about how we should reconfigure the world – about what a 'post-capitalist' world will be like – wearisome. I suspect a lot of it amounts to little more than a retreat into utopian fantasy among activists daunted by the power of capital and the state. I suspect it is a way of avoiding facing up to the real political task of building mass movements on the scale necessary to take on the rich, the banks, and the corporations.

So this is a book that focuses on just that. It is not utopian, because it describes the most powerful revolution from below in history; a moment when the common people, organised in their millions, marched onto the stage of history and took control of their own destiny. While it lasted, the Russian people 'stormed the heavens' – as Marx described the experience of the Paris Commune in 1871 – and showed the world what was possible when you did so. The Russian Revolution revealed the enormous potential for social transformation – for attempting to solve all of humanity's problems – inherent in mass popular democracy. It showed us what we can achieve when we take the power. But precisely because anti-capitalist revolution is, at this moment, despite being an imperative need, still only a distant possibility, the focus of the book is on the preparation for revolution as much as on the event and the aftermath.

PART ONE

The Spark, 1825–1916

CHAPTER ONE

The Regime

Medieval mysticism. Russian soldiers – peasants in uniform – kneel
as the Tsar passes by waving a holy icon.

The war was going badly, so the Tsar, the supreme ruler of 130 million Russians, had gone to the front to assume personal command. 'A new page begins, and only God Almighty knows what will be written on it', he announced. The Tsarina, who had stayed behind at the palace, wrote reassuringly: 'It will be a glorious page in your reign and Russian history.' He had nothing to fear, she added, because 'Our Friend's prayers arise night and day for you to Heaven, and God will hear them.' She reminded him that he had been supplied with a holy icon by this 'Friend' before setting out – 'to guard and guide you' – and later she sent an apple from the hands of the same, one Grigori Rasputin, a Siberian peasant faith-healer, urging her husband to eat it to strengthen his will. Rasputin was a drunkard, a lecher, and a charlatan. With a display of piety and a claim that he could cure her son's haemophilia, he had insinuated his way into the Court and become the Tsarina's closest advisor.[1]

When did this happen? A monarch going to war waving holy icons and eating sacred apples. Not in the twelfth century, but at the beginning of the twentieth.

Tsar Nicholas II, the last of the Romanovs, was a bloodless non-entity riddled with prejudice and superstition, a weak man paralysed by his own stupidity as the fires of war and revolution rose around him. His German wife, the Tsarina Alexandra, was equally benighted and gullible, yet more wilful. Men of talent were dismissed from Court and their places taken by fawning favourites, the appointees of the Alexandra/Rasputin clique, what one former minister called 'the leprous court camarilla'. In the shallow mind of the Tsarina, this was interpreted as strength. 'Being firm is the only saving', she told the Tsar. 'You are autocrat and they dare not forget it.' He was to 'crush them

---

1.   Trotsky 1932–3/1977, 85; Lincoln 1986, 160–1.

all', for he was 'the autocrat without which Russia cannot exist'. As this German aristocrat in a Russian palace explained it: 'Russia loves to feel the whip. That is her nature. Tender love, and then the iron hand to punish and guide.'[2] Thus did the last of the Romanovs meet the challenges of a world of railways, steelworks, and howitzers: with the barbarism of the Middle Ages.

How to explain this travesty? Georgi Plekhanov, the founder of the Russian socialist movement in the late nineteenth century, considered Russia 'too Europeanised in comparison with Asia, and inadequately Europeanised in comparison with Europe'.[3] It was, he implied, an historical hybrid which had entered the industrial age still saddled with an absolute monarch and a state-feudal social structure inherited from the sixteenth century.

To understand the revolution that exploded inside Russia in 1917, we must begin with a 'deep time' perspective – a sense, that is, of what the French historians of the *Annales* tradition call *la longue durée*. If revolution is 'compressed' history – the progress of a century becoming the achievement of a year – it becomes so only because long-accumulating contradictions have reached a critical mass.

The autocratic rule of the Tsars – and the militaristic manner in which Russia came to be ordered – was the result of the interaction of three factors: the backwardness of the economy; the weakness of civil society; and competition with rival powers. Let us consider this interaction in detail, for it provides the seed-bed of the revolutionary crisis to come.

---

2. Trotsky 1932–3/1977, 73–81; Lincoln 1986, 29.

3. Chamberlin 1935/1965, 2.

Old Russia

Tsarist Russia eventually comprised a vast territory of diverse geography, multiple ethnicities, and only the most rudimentary communications. It stretched from Poland and the Baltic Sea in the west to the Pacific Ocean in the east, from the icebound wastes of the Arctic in the north to the baking steppes of Central Asia in the south. The continental climate – cold in winter, hot in summer – was harsh. Great tracts of the country – the frozen tundra and taiga forest of the north – remained uncultivated wilderness. Much of the rest was poor land. The belt in which Moscow stands, the historic heart of Old Russia, where the taiga grades into mixed forest, is a region of sand and clay, bogs and marshes, with acidic soils low in humus. Further south again, where the woodland opens into vast expanses of steppe, lies the 'black earth' region, where the soil is better, but agriculture is hampered by unreliable rainfall, a short growing season, and, in the past, primitive technique.

Because land was plentiful but poor, Russian agriculture developed extensively: peasant pioneers from the old regions would trek into the wilderness to hack out new farms in successive waves of colonisation. Low yields also encouraged diversification: agriculture was supplemented by fur-trapping, fishing, bee-keeping, and cottage industries producing tools, household goods, clothes, icons, even musical instruments. Village people might be poor, but they were fairly self-sufficient.

This, combined with distance and lack of easy transport, meant that trade and towns were little developed. Most Russians lived in relative isolation. Civil society remained fragmented and unorganised.[4] The yeomanry and

4. Pipes 1974/1977, 3–22.

'mechanicals', the merchant-adventurers and industrial entrepreneurs, the classes of men that had pioneered the development of capitalism in north-west Europe between the sixteenth and eighteenth centuries, were largely absent in Old Russia. 'The meagreness not only of Russian feudalism, but of all the old Russian history,' wrote Leon Trotsky, who was both leader and historian of the Russian Revolution, 'finds its most depressing expression in the absence of real medieval cities as centres of commerce and craft.'[5]

The extreme centralisation of the Tsarist state was the flipside of Russian society's atomisation. The autocracy of the Tsar was made possible by the stagnation of urban life, the absence of culture, the void where strong public institutions had failed to develop. But instead of offering a paternal hand, Tsarism was like a brutal rider forcing forwards an overburdened mule; the state followed its own independent historical path, regarding the inert mass of humanity over which it presided as mere raw material for fashioning into a military machine. Under the pressure of geopolitical competition with rival powers, the Tsarist state became an end in itself. Its inner essence was politico-military accumulation: the amassing of manpower and military hardware as a means of empire-building. The Tsar did not exist to serve the people; they existed to serve him.

The last Tsar, Nicholas II, clung to this principle to the very end. With discontent rising all around him, isolated even within the Court itself, the British ambassador, Sir George Buchanan, asked the Tsar in late 1916 whether he should not make some effort to regain the confidence of his people. There was a long pause. Then Nicholas Romanov replied: 'Do you

---

5. Trotsky 1932–3/1977, 29.

mean that *I* am to regain the confidence of my people, or that they are to regain *my* confidence.'[6]

Because of primitive technique, rural poverty, and medieval infrastructure, only a regime of exceptional ruthlessness could accumulate the resources necessary to sustain the apparatus of global power. Russia's engine of war was fuelled by peasant muscle and blood. The method of extraction, from a hundred thousand villages spread across 5,000 miles, was necessarily crude and brutal.

The combination of backwardness and militarism gave to the Tsarist autocracy what Georgi Plekhanov and other contemporary Marxists considered an 'Asiatic' character. Russian history knew no Reformation, barely any Enlightenment, and only a most belated Industrial Revolution. Nothing compared with the Dutch, English, American, or French Revolutions. And in that great 'Springtime of Peoples' in 1848 – a rolling wave of popular insurrection sweeping through Paris, Berlin, Vienna, Budapest, and Rome – the Tsar, stepping forth as 'gendarme of Europe', employed his servile peasant-conscripts to shoot down the democratic revolutionaries on the barricades.

Militarism

The Russian tsars inherited much of their historic character from the Mongol khans. In the early thirteenth century, the Mongols had thundered across the steppes to create an empire that stretched the length of Asia. When their empire broke up in the later thirteenth century, a Mongol-Tartar

---

6. Lincoln 1986, 311.

(or Mongol-Turkic) khanate known as 'the Golden Horde' emerged in the north-western region of Central Asia. The princes of Moscow – protected somewhat by their location deep within the Russian hinterland, and enriched by the trade lines that ran through their territory – maintained a precarious semi-independence on the borders of the Golden Horde through craven submission to their Tartar overlords, serving them, in Marx's words, as 'hangman, sycophant, and slave-in-chief'. Then, as Tartar power waned, the princes of Moscow – formed in a mould of 'Asiatic' despotism, imbued with the instincts of the bully and the barbarian – took stage as masters in their own right.[7]

Landlocked, without defensible 'natural frontiers', surrounded by enemies, the embryonic state of Muscovy was compelled to fight for survival – and, eventually, supremacy – against the Tartar khanates of the disintegrating Golden Horde in the south-east, the feudal kingdom of Poland-Lithuania in the west, and the mercantile city-state of Novgorod in the north. The creation of a national state was mainly the work of Ivan the Great (1462–1505). During his reign, and that of his son, the territory of Muscovy increased six-fold. As it grew, a new class of dependent feudal landowners was created, men who held estates in return for service.[8] Yet greater conquests followed.

Ivan the Terrible (1533–84) was the first Muscovite ruler to proclaim himself Tsar ('Caesar'). So feared was he by his own people that they tolled the church bells to warn of his approach. A mentally deranged tyrant, he used mass murder

---

7. Kochan and Abraham 1962/1990, 22–8; Pipes 1974/1977, 54–64.
8. Kochan and Abraham 1962/1990, 29–40.

to create a centralised royal dictatorship and double the size of Muscovy from 2.8 to 5.4 million square miles. Novgorod lost its independence. Rival Slavic princes were struck down. And, equipped with cannon, muskets, and holy icons, the Orthodox Christian soldiers of the Tsar dispersed the Islamic horse-archers of the Golden Horde to push the boundaries of the state to the Ural Mountains and the Caspian Sea.

To support these wars of conquest, Ivan turned Muscovy into a military camp. The private estates of the *boyars* – the landowning nobility – were expropriated and became the personal property of the ruler. The Tsar was elevated into both proprietor and sovereign of a 'patrimonial' state. The nobility was organised into a service class of government officials and army officers. The peasantry, by legal diktat, lost its freedom and was reduced to serfdom, tied to the land and in thrall to the landlord, the tax-collector, and the recruiting sergeant. The towns, too, succumbed to the rising power of the autocracy. Novgorod was destroyed in 1570, its medieval timber buildings consumed by fire, its people hunted down and massacred in a bloody rampage that lasted for weeks.[9]

The terror almost brought matters to naught. The monstrous excesses of Ivan the Terrible provoked violent reaction after his death, a 'Time of Troubles', when usurpers and adventurers contested a vacant throne, popular rebels seized much of the countryside, and towns were sacked and villages burned by military freebooters. As Russia disintegrated internally, the Swedes took Novgorod, the Poles Moscow.

But as so often in its history when violated by foreign invasion, Russia found within itself unsuspected reserves of

9. Kochan and Abraham 1962/1990, 41–6; Pipes 1974/1977, 79–111.

strength. Behind the banners and icons of Orthodoxy, an army of liberation was raised. The Russians recaptured Moscow. Then a great assembly – the *Zemski Sobor* – was summoned to the Kremlin, and this, on 21 February 1613, proclaimed Michael Romanov the Tsar. The new dynasty would last for slightly more than 300 years.[10]

The rule of the Romanovs was based on the goon and the priest. Its watchwords were Autocracy, Orthodoxy, and Nationalism. The aristocracy had become a class of state officials. The peasants were scattered and enslaved. The towns were few and small. Trade was often state-controlled. Civil society was weak, apathetic, without enterprise or self-organisation. The active forces in Russian life – the forces that imparted dynamism to its inner processes – were the Tsarist state and the threat from foreign powers. So surpluses were hoovered upwards by a process of politico-military accumulation, draining it from towns and villages, which languished at a level of development grindingly medieval.

In the mid fifteenth century, when it was breaking free of the Golden Horde, Muscovy was about the size of Germany. By 1600, it had expanded to the size of the rest of Europe combined. By 1650, having absorbed Siberia, it was three times larger. In these two centuries, the Tsars of Russia gained territory equivalent to the size of Holland *every year*.[11]

By this time, however, parts of Europe were developing far more rapidly than Russia, and the modernisation and enlargement of the armed forces became a pressing imperative. Under Peter the Great (1682–1725), military expenditures consumed more than four-fifths of state revenue, the army

10.   Kochan and Abraham 1962/1990, 60–72.

11.   Pipes 1974/1977, 79–84.

swelled to a third of a million, and the state was at war every year bar one. The tax burden tripled. Conscription – of three recruits per thousand inhabitants – became an annual draft. State feudalism was bureaucratised: Tsar Peter's 'Table of Ranks' set out, in the manner of an Excel spread-sheet, a new 'Westernised' hierarchy of ranks, duties, and privileges. St Petersburg was founded as Russia's 'window on the West' – but it was done with the brutal forced-labour methods of Asiatic despotism. Tsarist Russia came to resemble a gigantic barracks, in which a military autocrat employed 100,000 landowners and 50,000 bureaucrats to tax, conscript, and police a hundred million peasants.[12]

In the Great Northern War (1700–21), Peter defeated Sweden, conquered the east coast of the Baltic, and turned Russia into one of Europe's great powers. Under Catherine the Great (1762–96), Russian expansionism surged again. The Kingdom of Poland was destroyed, and Russia, Prussia, and Austria partitioned it between them. The Ottoman-Turkish Empire was rolled back, and Russia seized territory in the Balkans, the Crimea, and the Caucasus. Then, between 1812 and 1814, Russia played a central role in the defeat of Napoleonic France, helping to inaugurate 30 years of reactionary 'throne and altar' politics in Europe.[13] Tsarist Russia henceforward formed, alongside Habsburg Austria, one of the two main pillars of conservatism on the continent. Surveying the prospects in early 1848, the young Frederick Engels declared that, in order to make the democratic

---

12.   Pipes 1974/1977, 112–29.

13.   Dupuy and Dupuy 1970, 614–7, 697–9, 756–63.

revolution, it would be necessary 'to fight the barbarian hordes of Austria and Russia'.[14]

Industrialisation

But the military machine was obsolescent by the mid nineteenth century. When wars were mainly a matter of masses of men, dragooned into line, bludgeoned forwards, Russia was well provided. The muskets and cannon needed to equip them were easy enough to turn out. These methods won the war of 1812, and still sufficed in wars of empire against Islamic khanates and Turkic tribesmen in the Caucasus and Central Asia as late as the 1860s and 1870s. The Tsar at this time was as pre-eminent an imperialist as any, pushing Russia's frontiers forwards until they met those of Persia, Afghanistan, and China.

But elsewhere, in conflict with other great powers, the Russian Imperial Army proved less formidable. Defeat in the Crimean War (1853–6) – fought on home territory against British and French invasion forces – revealed military weakness amounting to national crisis. Road and rail links to the front were virtually non-existent, the army's supply-line collapsed, and tens of thousands died unnecessarily of cold, disease, and hunger. The infantry were equipped with outdated muskets, so the prevailing military doctrine still favoured the bayonet over the bullet. Many officers were ignorant, corrupt, and brutal. The rank and file were sullen, cattle-like. The army was held together by ferocious discipline. The maximum number of lashes permitted was 6,000: a death sentence several times over. Leo Tolstoy, who fought in the Crimea, wrote that 'we

14.   Engels 1848/1973, 108.

have no army: we have a horde of slaves cowed by discipline, ordered about by thieves and slave-traders'.[15]

Reform was essential. Other parts of Europe were industrialising. Russia was not. The gap between the capitalist nation-states of Western Europe and the medieval empire of the Tsars was widening. By the late nineteenth century, great-power status depended on railways, howitzers, and machine-guns. To remain a great power, Russia had to have them, and that meant she had to have the coal mines, steelworks, and engineering plants to produce them. An industrial revolution had become a matter of national survival.

Lacking a sufficient stock of private capital, Russian economic development took a distinctive form. Under Sergei Witte, who held a succession of government economic posts between 1891 and 1903, the Tsarist state set about constructing an advanced military-industrial complex. As Witte complained in a confidential memorandum to the Tsar in 1899:

> The economic relationship of Russia to Western Europe is precisely similar to the relationship between colonial countries and their metropolises. But … Russia is a politically independent and mighty power; it has the right and the power not to want to pay tribute forever to the economically more advanced states … Russia wishes to be a metropolis itself.

Witte saw no alternative to large-scale state investment, with high taxes and foreign loans to fund it, and a protective wall of tariffs to keep out imports.

---

15. Goodlad 2015, 20–1.

Between 1892 and 1900, two-thirds of government spending was devoted to economic development, mainly railways, the principal driver of early twentieth-century industrialisation. The length of Russia's railway network doubled in less than 15 years. Pig-iron production almost trebled in ten. The overall industrial growth rate in the Witte years was 8 per cent per year: higher than that of any other major state at the time, and a phenomenal rate by any standards. By 1914, Russia ranked fifth in the world for industrial output, behind the US, Germany, Britain, and France, but ahead of Austria-Hungary, Italy, and Japan.

State debt spiralled, but the foreign loans to fund it poured in. French financiers in particular were more willing to lend in Russia than at home; Belgian, German, and British bankers also invested heavily. Foreigners may have supplied as much as a third of Russian capital in 1890, almost half by 1900. This flow of capital funded not only the railways and the heavy industries that supplied them – coal, iron, steel, machine-building – but other sectors too, like textiles, chemicals, oil. The number of weaving spindles in Russia, for example, increased by three-quarters between 1890 and 1900.[16]

Russia's new industries were of the most advanced kind. Such large-scale investment meant big modern factories and cutting-edge technology. Russian capitalism was able to leap the early phases of industrialisation in a single bound. Thus, by 1914, whereas small enterprises of less than 100 workers still employed 35 per cent of US factory workers, they employed only 18 per cent of their Russian counterparts. By contrast,

16. Kochan 1967/1970, 24–31; Kochan and Abraham 1962/1990, 226–9; Pipes 1974/1977, 192–3.

giant enterprises of 1,000 or more employed 18 per cent in the US and no less than 41 per cent in Russia.

These new industries were concentrated in a handful of economic zones. Two-thirds of Russia's industrial workers were employed in just three hotspots: St Petersburg (metallurgy, machinery, armaments), Moscow (textiles, metal-processing, chemicals), and the Ukrainian Donbass (coal, iron, chemicals). Also important were Russian Poland (textiles, coal, iron, chemicals), the Urals (mining, metallurgy), and Baku (oil).[17]

On the other hand, the industrial sector as a whole remained relatively small; some four-fifths of Russians still worked on the land, compared with less than a third in the US. Despite the boom, Russian infrastructure and output were still dwarfed by those of Imperial Germany, the fast-rising titan of European capitalism. On the eve of war in 1914, Germany's railway density was 30 times greater than Russia's; even Austria-Hungary's was 18 times greater. Early twentieth-century Tsarist Russia was a mixture of the most advanced technique and primeval backwardness: an extreme example of what Trotsky called 'combined and uneven development'.[18]

It was not simply that the new industries made a contrast with a vast, languid, primitive countryside. Tradition and modernity interpenetrated everywhere; the entire social order was destabilised as market forces eroded the solidarity of the village, uprooted young peasants, and cast them into the mines, mills, and metal-works of Russia's exploding slum-cities. The central contradiction of Tsarism – between, on the one hand, the great-power status of the regime and its geopolitical imperatives, and, on the other, the relative underdevelopment

17.   Trotsky 1932–3/1977, 31–2; Kochan 1967/1970, 35.
18.   Trotsky 1932–3/1977, 31; Cliff 1989, 128.

of economy, society, and culture – yawned wider as Russia commenced its belated, catch-up industrial revolution. In 1905, the contradiction exploded into crisis, as military defeat in the Far East detonated proletarian revolution in Europe.

The 1905 Revolution

Russian imperialism's three pressure-points were the Black Sea, Central Asia, and the Far East. Pushing against the decaying Ottoman Empire, Russia's advance in the Black Sea region had been blocked by combinations of other European powers, during both the Crimean War of 1853–6 and the Russo-Turkish War of 1877–8. The conquest of Central Asia had also come up against a barrier: here, through the nineteenth century, among the petty potentates of Persian steppes and Afghan mountains, Britain and Russia played out a diplomatic 'Great Game' whose outcome was stalemate. The Far East appeared to offer better prospects.

The 'Scramble for China' was well underway by the late nineteenth century, as rival powers hacked off chunks of the ancient empire's territory ('concessions' in the diplomatic language of the time) to found a string of coastal trading ports. The magnetic pull of easy pickings in northern China drew the attention of Tsarist statesmen, and the Trans-Siberian Railway was constructed across Manchuria to Vladivostok. But the port was ice-bound three months a year and gave direct access only to the Sea of Japan, from which passage to the Pacific was through the narrow and easily defended Straits of Tsushima. The supreme prize was Port Arthur on the Liaotung Peninsula: a warm-water port on the Yellow Sea.[19]

---

19.   Connaughton 2003, 11–15.

But there was a rival for influence here. In the war of 1894–5, exploiting (and laying bare) China's weakness, the Japanese had bludgeoned their way into Korea, Manchuria, and Port Arthur. At the time, the threat of combined naval action by Russia, Germany, and France had forced the Japanese to disgorge their gains. The Russians had then filled the vacuum, obtaining a lease on Port Arthur, building a rail link with the Trans-Siberian, and pushing troops into Manchuria and Korea. Meantime, the Japanese had embarked on a crash programme of ship-building. Eight years later they were ready, and on 8 February 1904 they renewed the struggle for northern China by attacking the Russian forces holding Port Arthur.[20]

The war was a disaster for the Russians. The Japanese forces were efficient, up-to-date, and highly motivated. They were also fully mobilised in a war fought close to home. The Russians, by contrast, could deploy only part of their strength, and had to operate at the end of a 5,000-mile railway line. Local transport and supplies were inadequate, officers corrupt and incompetent, troops badly equipped, tactics antiquated. The Siberian peasant-soldier was tough but neither resourceful nor enthusiastic. The Tsarist assumption that Japan was a second-rate Asian power turned out to be groundless. After a succession of shattering victories on land which hurled the Russians out of Port Arthur and back 250 miles north of the Yellow Sea, the Japanese annihilated the Russian Baltic Fleet – just arrived after a voyage of seven months – at the Battle of Tsushima on 27 May 1905.[21] Well before this, awakened by news of defeat in the East, revolution had broken out in the West.

---

20.   Kochan and Abraham 1962/1990, 248; Connaughton 2003, 16–24.
21.   Dupuy and Dupuy 1970, 920–6; Connaughton 2003, 25–36.

'We need a small victorious war to stem the tide of revolution', Prime Minister Plehve had announced when the war against Japan began.[22] In the event, as Trotsky observed, the war 'drastically speeded up the natural process of destruction of the autocracy'.[23] Military defeat and political agitation intermeshed in the autumn of 1904 as middle-class liberals ratcheted up a campaign for constitutional reform in the face of an intransigent regime. In December came the news that Port Arthur had fallen to the Japanese. And on 9 January, the working class of St Petersburg entered the political fray. Marching from four or five assembly points in the suburbs, the workers converged on the Winter Palace in the centre of the city, perhaps 200,000 strong, the biggest demonstration in Russian history. Led by Father Gapon – a simple priest, part gullible tool of the Tsarist police, part well-meaning man of the people – they were wearing their Sunday best, singing hymns, and carrying portraits of the Tsar and icons of the Virgin. A black thronging mass standing in the snow, they had come to petition their 'Little Father' for redress of grievance.

Then it began: Bloody Sunday. The Cossacks – cavalry armed with carbines and sabres – charged into the crowd, hacking down men, women, and children. As people fled, they ran into rolling volleys from lines of Guardsmen. In places, the panic-stricken crowd was corralled and cut down where it stood. Elsewhere, sporadic killing spilled down the streets around the Winter Palace. No-one is sure how many died, but it was probably more than a thousand.[24]

22. Cliff 1975/1986, 139.

23. Glatter 2005, 42.

24. Chamberlin 1935/1965, 47–9; Kochan 1967/1970, 91–2.

The following day, 125,000 St Petersburg workers went on strike in protest at the massacre. From that moment, though it ebbed and flowed, a gigantic movement of mass strikes and demonstrations, of peasant insurrections, and of military mutinies surged across Russia. It reached its climax that autumn. For 50 days, from mid October to early December, the Tsarist capital was virtually ruled by the St Petersburg Soviet of Workers' Deputies, a strike committee which had evolved into a revolutionary assembly representing some 200,000 workers. The regime was hammered by a mass strike in St Petersburg in October, another in November, and then armed insurrection in Moscow in early December.

But the movement could not break through, and the regime counterattacked. During October, around 3,500 people had been killed in anti-Semitic pogroms organised by the secret police and right-wing paramilitaries known as 'Black Hundreds'. In early December, the St Petersburg Soviet was suppressed and its leaders arrested; the proletarian suburbs of Moscow were shelled and prisoners shot down in cold blood. Then, punitive expeditions were dispatched to regions of national revolt and peasant insurrection – to Poland, the Caucasus, and the Baltic provinces; to Siberia and the black-earth regions of Central and European Russia. The toll eventually reached 15,000 dead, 18,000 wounded, and 79,000 imprisoned. The retreating movement collapsed under the blows of the Tsarist terror. In 1905, there had been 24 million strike-days in Russia; by 1908, it was less than a million.[25]

Lenin described 1905 as Russia's great 'dress-rehearsal'. So it was. On the stage of war and revolution, the rottenness

---

25. Serge 1930/1972, 40–1; Chamberlin 1935/1965, 49–58; Kochan 1967/1970, 86–114; Cliff 1989, 88–116.

of Tsarism had been laid bare, and the full cast of players in the drama of its destruction had appeared – the liberal bourgeoisie, the peasantry, the workers, the soldiers and sailors, and the political parties, some revolutionary, some not so revolutionary.

Though the millions stirred into motion by the heady events of 1905 lapsed back into the apathetic routines of everyday life, they had been changed. A river of blood now divided regime and people. Never again would a working-class demonstration parade behind the symbols of Tsarism and Orthodoxy. And among the people, embedded especially in the ranks of the urban proletariat, were thousands of activists who, though demoralised and disorganised, had been transformed by the experience of 1905 into the cadre of a much more extensive revolutionary underground.

Not just a dress-rehearsal, then: also a university. And as little groups of defeated revolutionaries came together, meeting secretly in apartments in the workers' districts, or in foreign towns where as exiles they had taken refuge, they discussed the significance of what had happened, and debated what had gone wrong.

None more so than those who called themselves 'Social Democrats' (though today we would call them 'revolutionary socialists'). About two things there was wide agreement: that the St Petersburg movement had exhausted itself and subsided before the Moscow workers were fully mobilised; and that the soldiers – peasants in uniform – had remained loyal to the regime.[26]

Beyond this, however, the Social Democrats agreed on little. Having been welded together in the fires of 1905, they

---

26. Serge 1930/1972, 41–3.

now splintered into fragments as the fires went out; and then slowly reformed around three distinct positions. The century-old riddle of Russian history – what form must the anti-Tsarist revolution take in order to be victorious? – was now reconfigured in the light of white-hot experience. The one who grasped it best – the inner dynamic of the drama-to-come as revealed in its dress-rehearsal – was the man who more than any other embodied its living spirit: the 25-year-old Jewish intellectual Leon Trotsky, the effective leader of the short-lived St Petersburg Soviet. But his was, for long, a minority voice. To understand why, we must delve deep into the murky world of Russian revolutionary politics between 1825 and 1917.

CHAPTER TWO

The Revolutionaries

Bloody Sunday. The Tsar's soldiers shoot down demonstrators
outside the Winter Palace in St Petersburg in 1905.

Revolutions always take the world by surprise. Often, the revolutionaries themselves – always a small minority before the revolution actually begins – are the most surprised of all. And always, the revolution confounds expectations: it invariably plays out differently from the way in which revolutionaries imagined it would. The great German philosopher Georg Hegel – who inspired Marx – remarked that 'The owl of Minerva spreads its wings only with the coming of the dusk.' He meant that wisdom follows from experience; first is the deed, then the understanding. So it was with the Russian Revolution.

Until it happened, hardly anyone could figure out how it would happen – even though anti-Tsarist revolutionaries had been debating the issue for almost a century. However, the false preconceptions mattered, because they affected how people acted when the revolution finally arrived. Things then unfolded very quickly, and people struggled to think clearly amid the profusion of events and cacophony of opinions. So they fell back on prior assumptions. Unable to keep pace with the *actual* revolution, they acted according to their preconceived notion of how the revolution *ought* to be. In this way, old ideas that did not correspond to real experience became a barrier to progress. To understand the clash of rival factions during 1917, therefore, it is useful to know something of the prehistory of the Russian revolutionary movement.

The first blow in the century-long struggle between Tsarism and the Russian *Narod* ('people') had been struck on 14 December 1825. There was a new tsar, Nicholas I, and the soldiers were to take their oath of allegiance in St Petersburg's Senate Square. That allegiance was contested, and for some six hours loyalist and rebel soldiers confronted one another across the open space. Then, as the sun went down, the rebels having rejected a summons to surrender, cannon were trained on them and the square was finally cleared. The Decembrist Revolt had collapsed with hardly a shot fired. About 600 conspirators were later investigated. Of these, five were hanged and a hundred or so exiled to Siberia.

Colonel Paul Pestel, one of the Decembrist leaders, said of their failure that 'We wanted the harvest before we had sown.' The British minister in St Petersburg concurred, writing, in an analysis that was both accurate and prophetic, that 'The late conspiracy failed for want of management, and want of a head to direct it, and was too premature to answer any good purpose, but I think the seeds are sown which one day will produce important consequences.'

Though the eighteenth-century Russian Enlightenment had been a shallow affair, noble officers campaigning against Napoleon had been brought face-to-face with the relative backwardness of their own society. They found themselves commanding an army of serfs and fighting an army of citizen-soldiers. And when they followed the retreating French into the heart of Europe, marching eventually into Paris itself, they saw a new world in the making. So they began plotting for change. And being officers and gentlemen, they imagined that an aristocratic conspiracy would suffice. The abolition of serfdom and a republican constitution were to be achieved by a military coup. The Decembrist Revolt was the failed revolution of men like Leo Tolstoy's character Pierre Bezukhov in *War and Peace*: idealists with a sense of *noblesse oblige*.

The conspirators were a minority of their class, and lacked support from other classes. Even their own ranks were shaky: they haemorrhaged defectors, and then hesitated in the breach that fateful December day.[1] But they were not forgotten. 'From a spark a flame will flare up', wrote one of the exiled Decembrists in reply to a sympathetic poem addressed to them by Alexander Pushkin. And in 1900, when Russian Social Democrats founded a revolutionary newspaper, they called it *Iskra* – 'The Spark' – because they looked back in admiration to their Decembrist forebears. Grigori Zinoviev, a leading Bolshevik, considered them 'the cream of the aristocracy', men who had 'detached themselves from their class, broken from their families, abandoned privileges, and joined battle with the autocracy'.[2]

The radical intelligentsia

In the wake of the failed revolt, Russian radicalism retreated into the intimacy of the salon. It was the currency of the intelligentsia – writers, professional men, liberal bourgeois, young nobles – not yet of the common people. Alexander Herzen (1812–70) was one its brightest stars. To find the freedom to speak out, he chose permanent exile. He was in Paris during the 1848 Revolution, and his magazine, *The Bell*, which circulated inside Russia, was later published in London. When radical students were expelled from St Petersburg University, he wrote to tell them where they should go:

> From all corners of our enormous land, from the Don and the Ural, from the Volga and the Dnieper, a moan is growing, a grumbling is rising. This is the first roar of the sea-billow, which begins to rage, pregnant with storm, after a long and

1. Kochan and Abraham 1962/1990, 152–60.

2. Zinoviev 1923/1973, 17, 71.

tiresome calm. *V Narod*. To the people. That is your place,
O exiles of knowledge.[3]

Here was an idea: to the *Narod*. And Herzen's cry would call
forth a generation of revolutionaries with just that aim: the
Narodniks.

Nikolai Chernyshevsky (1828–89) was another icon of
radicalism. Arrested in 1862 and incarcerated for almost two
years in the Peter and Paul Fortress, a grim Tsarist prison in
St Petersburg, he there wrote his greatest work, *What is to
be Done?* He was then sent to hard labour in Siberia for 20
years. Chernyshevsky represented a change of tone in the
radical intelligentsia. The 'men of the forties', like Herzen, had
been liberal romantics, whereas the 'men of the sixties' were
social revolutionaries. 'I do not like those gentlemen who say
"Liberty! Liberty!" and do not destroy a social order under
which nine-tenths of the people are slaves and proletarians',
wrote the young Chernyshevsky in his diary. 'The important
thing is not whether there is a tsar or not, whether there is
a constitution or not, but that one class should not suck the
blood of another.'[4]

Though only a minor character in *What is to be Done?*,
Rakhmetov, a renegade young noble, became a role model
for two generations of Russian revolutionaries. Seeking to be
'loved and esteemed by the common people', he was an extreme
ascetic, eating only simple food, working as a barge-hauler,
avoiding drink, and remaining celibate. He read voraciously,
but chose only original works, and was deliberately brusque of

3.   Chamberlin 1935/1965, 22–3.
4.   Chamberlin 1935/1965, 25–7.

manner to avoid wasting time on formalities and trivia. Chernyshevsky presents Rakhmetov as a new and special type:

> They are few in number, but through them the life of all mankind expands; without them it would have been stifled. They are few in number, but they put others in a position to breathe, who without them would have been suffocated. Great is the mass of good and honest men, but Rakhmetovs are rare. They are the best among the best, they are the movers of movers, they are the salt of the salt of the earth.[5]

Chernyshevsky's image of the revolutionary as heroic champion of the people appealed to his readers because it idealised their own situation. In the distant past, the peasants had risen in revolt under leaders of their own class – under Razin in the 1670s, Bulavin in the 1700s, Pugachev in the 1770s. But between the defeat of Pugachev in 1775 and the outbreak of revolution in 1905, there were no peasant revolts in Russia. The popular movements of the eighteenth century had lacked leadership: but the radical intelligentsia of the nineteenth century lacked a movement.

The intelligentsia is not a class. A class is formed by economic processes and social relationships centred on exploitation. The intelligentsia is merely a social layer defined by occupation, education, and lifestyle. Mass mobilisation of an entire social class – the peasantry or the proletariat (the industrial working class) – can transform society. The intelligentsia has no such power. Because it is concerned with the creation and dissemination of ideas, it may generate critiques that give expression to a range of discontents, especially where

5.   Chernyshevsky 1863/1961, ix-xviii, 221–61, esp. 241.

the institutions of civil society – as opposed to those of the state – are underdeveloped. The intellectuals can then become – or imagine themselves to have become – 'the voice of the people'. But critique, however trenchant, cannot be acted upon unless it connects with social forces powerful enough to overcome the resistance of vested interests. This was the impasse confronting Russia's radical intelligentsia throughout the nineteenth century.

For sure, the number of professionally trained persons was rising – with the expansion of both the state bureaucracy and the industrial economy, from some 20,000 to 85,000 between 1860 and 1900. Almost 50,000 of these were eventually employed by local government institutions (the *zemstva*) as teachers, doctors, engineers, agronomists, and statisticians. To meet the demand for professional labour, turn-of-the-century Russia had 52 institutions of higher education and 25,000 enrolled students. This enlarged intelligentsia met in the *zemstva*, the colleges, and numerous semi-clandestine discussion 'circles', where they debated the polemics published in a plethora of radical periodicals known as 'fat journals'.[6]

But there was no unified view in this intermediate social layer. Nobility and intelligentsia overlapped, especially in a country where the landowning class traditionally dominated state service. The upper echelons of government were still aristocratic, the bureaucracy was organised in a rigid hierarchy of ranks and titles, and most men of education, irrespective of social origin, sought advancement within this framework. Many, unsurprisingly, were out-and-out reactionaries, espousing a mystical conservative-nationalist Pan-Slavism, which translated in practice into support for Tsarism,

6. Pipes 1974/1977, 261–5.

Russian Orthodoxy, and the 'Black Hundreds' (semi-official paramilitary bands of anti-Semitic thugs). These, for sure, were a minority, but most members of the elite, whether noble or bourgeois, were moderates; at best, they might be anti-Tsarist liberals who advocated parliamentary government.[7] This strand in Russian life would eventually find its main political expression in the Constitutional Democratic Party (the Cadets), a liberal bourgeois organisation founded in 1905. Only a minority of Russian intellectuals favoured social revolution. But it was among this group that debate raged about how the autocracy could be overthrown and Russia transformed. And it was from this group that virtually all senior revolutionary leaders emerged.

Most of the radicals were Narodniks ('Populists'). Russia, even in 1914, remained predominantly a country of agriculture and peasants, and the traditional, pre-capitalist village commune (the *mir*) seemed to offer a model for wider social reform. The Narodnik vision was of a peasant revolution to overthrow the Tsar, the landlords, and the priests, and of a post-revolutionary utopia based on villages, free farms, and local production.

But how were the dark masses of the Russian countryside – the peasants (*muzhiks* in Russian) – to be stirred into action? In 1874, about 2,500 radicals literally 'went to the people', travelling into the countryside, often wearing peasant dress, to agitate among villagers for revolution. Some – like those who immediately denounced the Tsar or denied God – were reported to the authorities. Others – focusing on economic grievances – got a better hearing. But that was all: no organisation was built, no struggle sparked. Even so, the

---

7. Fitzpatrick 1982/1984, 16–17.

authorities took no chances, treating the whole movement as an attempted revolution, and by the autumn they had more than 1,500 young people under arrest. A second 'going to the people' the following year had similar results.[8]

Other methods were attempted. On 6 December 1876, a small demonstration – probably no more than a few hundred – assembled in front of Kazan Cathedral in St Petersburg to hear a young student called Georgi Plekhanov deliver a speech and unfurl a red banner inscribed 'Land and Liberty'. Among those present were advocates of 'propaganda of the deed'. Frustrated by the inertness of the villages, they argued for campaigns of terrorism to jump-start the revolution. Their thinking was muddled, but the gist was that terrorism would destabilise the state, expose its weakness and repressive character, and inspire the peasants with examples of heroic action. The Kazan Cathedral demonstration was, of course, broken up by the police. 'Land and Liberty' then became the name of a secret underground organisation. But the group soon split. The supporters of 'Black Partition' argued for propaganda in the countryside, but this faction soon faded away. The supporters of 'People's Will' (*Narodnya Volya*), on the other hand, about 200 strong, carried out a series of high-profile assassinations, culminating in a bomb attack which killed Tsar Alexander II in 1881.[9]

It did not work. The *modus operandi* of terrorists requires them, in the interests of security, to cut their links with the masses, who, even if they approve, are left mere spectators. The state, on the other hand, can use 'outrages' to justify intensified repression against all forms of opposition. So

8.   Kochan and Abraham 1962/1990, 215–6.
9.   Serge 1930/1972, 25–6; Kochan and Abraham 1962/1990, 216–19.

it was now. Even the assassination of a tsar failed to trigger revolution. What it did instead was to give the government its excuse for constructing a fully fledged police state during the following decade. All political activity was effectively banned, and a greatly expanded police apparatus was granted unlimited powers of surveillance, search, arrest, interrogation, imprisonment, and exile to deal with 'crimes against the state'. To help track down tiny numbers of revolutionaries, the work, movements, and pastimes of ordinary citizens were made dependent on official authorisation and hedged around with restrictions. To stop a handful of gunmen, nothing was to be permitted to any of Russia's 130 million inhabitants without a licence, a passport, or a government stamp.[10]

The most heroic of the intelligentsia had tried to bring down Tsarism with a proclamation and a bomb. All they had achieved was to conjure a police state that destroyed them. The *muzhik* masses they had wished to rouse remained in political slumber. Why was this?

The peasantry

Peasant life was shaped by agricultural routine and social isolation. The long, cold winter was spent largely indoors, in family log-cabins warmed by earthen stoves, doing craftwork and repairs, resting and sleeping, telling stories, getting drunk. Spring would come suddenly with the thaw, the ice breaking on the rivers, the waters flooding across the fields, the frozen land turning green in their wake. Then, through the short growing season from April to September, toil was relentless. Typically, Russian peasants operated a three-year cycle, one

10.   Pipes 1974/1977, 305–13.

field sown with spring oats, a second with winter rye, a third left fallow: a primitive, low-yield, medieval system.[11]

The villages were haunted by poverty, hunger, and disease. Horses provided the sole source of power, yet in the 1880s one-quarter of the peasants did not own one: they were forced to pull their own ploughs. 'Your majesty has 130 million subjects', Witte wrote to the Tsar in 1898. 'Of them, barely more than half can live; the rest vegetate.' As a 1905 police report explained: 'Very often the peasants do not have enough allotment land, and cannot during the year feed themselves, clothe themselves, heat their homes, keep their tools and livestock, secure seed for sowing, and, lastly, discharge all their taxes and obligations to the state, the *zemstvo*, and the commune.'[12]

The joint family and the village commune constituted almost the whole of the peasant's social ambit, one in which he submerged his own identity, and from the security of which he viewed the outside world with suspicion. Most were loyal to their 'Little Father', who would surely receive them warmly if they took their complaints to the palace, and would be as angry as they if only he knew the injustices perpetrated by landlords and officials in his name. The more devout found adequate expression for their weary fatalism in the rituals of Russian Orthodoxy, all incense, icons, and ignorance. Most could not read, and few journals in any case reached the villages. The more broken-spirited took to the bottle.[13] Little wonder that the Narodnik missionaries of the early 1870s, exotic creatures from another world, had hit a wall.

---

11. Pipes 1974/1977, 141–4.

12. Kochan 1967/1970, 57–8.

13. Pipes 1974/1977, 155–62.

Yet there was brooding discontent in the hearts of the *muzhiks*. Serfdom had been abolished in 1861, and the authorities' fear of revolt had been a motive. 'It is better to abolish serfdom from above than to wait for the time when it will begin to abolish itself from below', Tsar Alexander II had explained to a gathering of Moscow notables in 1856. Another motive was the lamentable condition of the Russian armed forces. In the wake of the disastrous Crimean War, the Tsarist state had urgent need to raise the quality of its military conscripts: browbeaten serfs made bad soldiers.[14]

But the hopes of peasants for a better life – for both the abolition of serfdom and a 'Black Partition' that would give every man a decent-sized farm – were dashed. The Emancipation Edict turned out to be a landlord's charter. Nobility, gentry, and rich farmers retained two-thirds of the land, including most pasture and woodland. The result was that in European Russia, while the 30,000 richest families owned 76 million hectares, some 10.5 million peasant households owned only a fraction more, 82 million, between them. Even the one-third allocated to the peasants had to be paid for. The government advanced 80 per cent of the cost to the landlords, but required the peasants to pay this back in the form of 'redemption payments' over a period of 49 years. The remaining 20 per cent of the purchase price was paid directly to the landlords by the peasants in money or in kind. In consequence, the post-emancipation peasantry was crippled by both land shortage and debt repayment. Most, therefore, remained in thrall to big landowners, the politico-juridical compulsion of serfdom now replaced by economic compulsion. The effect was to deepen the poverty of the villages. Chronic undernour-

14.   Kochan and Abraham 1962/1990, 182.

ishment raised the death rate by almost a third between 1800 and 1880. Travellers in the Russian countryside around 1900 found the *muzhik* sullen and hostile.[15]

The abolition of serfdom had another effect: it hastened the development of capitalist farming, widening the division in the villages between a minority of rich peasants (*kulaks*) and the rest. The process was analysed by the Russian revolutionary Vladimir Lenin in *The Development of Capitalism in Russia* (1898). One in five peasants, he observed, constituted a rural 'petty-bourgeoisie' (a class of small-business owners); these were evolving into a class of capitalist farmers. They had large farms, often supplemented by rented land, well supplied with horses (for traction), cattle (for manure), and farm implements (like metal ploughs); and they would often hire additional labour at busy times. Fully half the peasants, by contrast, owned too little property for even basic subsistence. They were forced to rent land, hire out their labour, supplement income with craftwork, or join the great southward migration of poor labourers each spring in search of work on the commercial estates of the Ukraine. For Lenin, 'the real trend of economic development of the peasant members of village communes is precisely in the direction of the creation of a rural bourgeoisie [a class of big-business owners] and of forcing the mass of the poorest farmers into the ranks of the proletariat [a class of wage-labourers]'. Instead of the village commune being a short-cut to socialism, as the Narodniks envisaged, 'the new economic organism which is emerging from the shell of serfdom in Russia is commercial agriculture and capitalism'.[16]

---

15. Lenin 1908/undated, 148; Kochan and Abraham 1962/1990, 193;
     Pipes 1974/1977, 164–8.

16. Lenin 1898/undated, 200, 207, 231–2, and passim.

Others, too, noticed this trend. But where Lenin detected revolutionary potential in the emerging rural proletariat, the Tsar's ministers identified potential allies in the peasant petty-bourgeoisie. With the spring thaw in 1905, the peasants had joined the revolution, looting and burning estates, seizing the land they had been so long denied. Once order was restored, the government undertook a belated agrarian reform, abolishing redemption payments, allowing peasants to consolidate holdings and leave the commune, and providing funds for the purchase of additional land. The village thereby lost control over land and labour as peasant farms were privatised and deregulated. Instead of communal control over pasture and woodland, and periodic redistribution of arable, farms became the exclusive private property of individual peasants. Altogether 12 million peasant households and 130 million hectares were involved. By 1916, independent peasants owned two-thirds of the cultivated land in private possession in European Russia, had leases on most of the rest, and held 90 per cent of the livestock.[17] Stolypin, the minister chiefly responsible for this policy, was, according to Lenin, attempting 'a bourgeois evolution of the landlord type'; his aim was 'to turn the old autocracy into a bourgeois monarchy' by providing the Tsar with a base of support among a new class of agrarian entrepreneurs.[18]

He failed (and Lenin misjudged how far he had got). The peasants gained confidence and strength from the concessions won in 1905, and they would join the revolution in 1917 to finish the business, seizing the forests of the state, the fields of the big landlords, and the warehouses of the commercial

---

17. Kochan and Abraham 1962/1990, 270–1; Pipes 1974/1977, 169.
18. Kochan 1967/1970, 142.

estates – liquidating, that is, remaining large-scale property in rural Russia.[19] Instead of the village being divided against itself, rich peasants against the rest, locked in a new, modern kind of class war, it marched as one to settle old scores inherited from the feudal past. The middle peasants still had land and wanted more. The poor peasants dreamed of a farm of their own. Neither Stolypin's attempted 'embourgeoisement' of the rich peasants nor Lenin's imagined 'proletarianisation' of the poor had yet fractured the medieval solidarity of the village.

Russia's peasants were still, as Marx had once described those of France, 'a sack of potatoes': not a collective *per se*, but a mass of individuals bound together as a class by the actuality or the hope of petty-proprietorship.

> In so far as millions of families live under economic conditions of existence that separate their mode of life, their interests, and their cultural formation from those of the other classes, and bring them into conflict with those classes, they form a class. In so far as these small peasant proprietors are merely connected on a local basis, and the identity of their interests fails to produce a feeling of community, national links, or a political organisation, they do not form a class. They are therefore incapable of asserting their class interest in their own name ... They cannot represent themselves; they must be represented.[20]

The peasants were the overwhelming majority of Russian society, but they were scattered, isolated, and parochial in outlook. They were capable of revolutionary action: 1905 had proved that. But they considered their revolution complete

---

19. Pipes 1974/1977, 169.
20. Marx 1852/1869/1973, 238–9.

when they had seized the land and divided it up. And if the towns remained unconquered, the Tsarist state would survive; and in that case, sooner or later, the soldiers would come to 'restore order' in the villages. Successful revolution required centralised national leadership. Who was to provide this?

The Social Democrats

Peasant revolt was an essential condition of the Russian Revolution. Without it, the army, formed overwhelmingly of peasant-conscripts, would remain loyal and shoot down the revolutionaries. But it was not a sufficient condition, for peasants, an amalgam of petty-proprietors rather than a class collective, could not create their own revolutionary party and leadership. They had to be led from the outside – by the towns.

The Narodniks had grappled unsuccessfully with this problem. While exaggerating the revolutionary potential of the peasantry, and the socialist character of the village commune, they had imagined themselves, a small party of radical intellectuals, as sufficient to trigger a peasant land-war, either by speeches or direct action. By the early 1880s, under intensified police crackdown, it was clear they had failed. And some of the Narodniks of the 1870s now became the Social Democrats of the 1880s. The most important of these was Georgi Plekhanov, who, in 1883, founded the Emancipation of Labour Group in St Petersburg and, also that year, published the first major work of Russian Marxism, *Socialism and the Political Struggle*.[21]

All Social Democrats – as socialists in general tended to be known a century ago – were agreed that the coming revolution would not be led by the countryside, but by the towns. Beyond

21. Cliff 1975/1986, 25.

that, however, there was disagreement. Most believed that Russia's backwardness meant that only 'bourgeois revolution' was possible. It would – so the argument went – overthrow Tsarism, establish parliamentary democracy and civil liberties, and sweep away the survivals of feudalism in town and country. Capitalism would then develop rapidly, creating the preconditions, in the long run at least, for a further revolution to achieve socialism. But who would lead this initial 'bourgeois revolution'? Two factions emerged around this question.

The more moderate – known as 'Mensheviks' – argued that the liberal bourgeoisie, represented after 1905 by the Cadet Party, would spearhead the struggle against Tsarism, and that it was the job of Social Democrats to support them, while avoiding any 'excesses' or 'extremism' that might fracture the class alliance between (liberal) capitalists and (socialist) workers. 'Therefore,' argued the Mensheviks, 'Social Democracy must not aim at seizing or sharing power in the provisional government, but must remain the party of the extreme revolutionary opposition.' To do otherwise, to seek state power itself, would be disastrous, because the Social Democrats 'would not be able to satisfy the pressing needs of the working class, including the establishment of socialism, ... and ... would cause the bourgeois classes to recoil from the revolution and thus diminish its sweep'.[22]

The more radical faction – known as 'Bolsheviks' – argued the opposite, claiming that the Russian bourgeoisie was small, weak, heavily dependent on Tsarism and foreign capital, and, as a class of big property-owners, terrified by the prospect of revolutionary upheaval; consequently, the revolution, albeit necessarily 'bourgeois' in its immediate historic purpose,

22.   Cliff 1975/1986, 197.

would have to be led by the working class in alliance with the peasantry. 'The only force capable of gaining a decisive victory over Tsarism', declared Lenin in *Two Tactics of Social Democracy in the Democratic Revolution* (1905), 'is the people, i.e. the proletariat and the peasantry ... The revolution's decisive victory over Tsarism means the establishment of the revolutionary-democratic dictatorship of the proletariat and the peasantry.'[23]

The phraseology was unfortunate. It had been the common practice of revolutionaries since the time of Marx, however, to describe any form of people power as a 'dictatorship'. The implication was neither autocracy nor even minority rule; on the contrary, all revolutionaries were democrats. The term was used to express the idea that the majority – the working people organised democratically – would have to impose their will on the defeated ruling classes by force. But there was a far greater problem with Lenin's formulation, 'the revolutionary-democratic dictatorship of the proletariat and the peasantry': the logic was tortuous. He seemed to be saying that only the workers and peasants could be relied upon, but having made the revolution, it would be the bourgeoisie – the capitalist class – that would end up in charge and reap most of the benefit.

He was, however, right about one thing: in 1905, at the first sound of gunfire, the Cadets had run for cover. At the beginning of the year, leading Cadet Peter Struve had declared that 'every sincere and thinking liberal in Russia demands revolution'. By its end, in the wake of the October-November mass strikes, he spoke instead of 'the pernicious anarchy of the Russian revolution'.[24]

---

23.   Cliff 1975/1986, 198.
24.   Cliff 1975/1986, 146–7.

But there is no question that Lenin's formulation, however accurate its assessment of the bourgeoisie's timidity, harboured a contradiction. Why would the workers, if they were to lead the revolution, impose upon themselves and their peasant allies a self-denying ordinance, handing over the power they had won to their class enemies, restricting themselves to the democratic reforms permitted by 'bourgeois revolution', postponing socialism to some distant and uncertain future?

It was the young Leon Trotsky, almost alone among Russian revolutionaries, who grasped the full implications of 1905.[25] His point of departure was the unity of the world, and the way in which economic and political competition had forced Tsarism into a belated attempt to catch up through a programme of rapid industrialisation funded by the state and foreign banks. The result was an exceptionally extreme example of 'combined and uneven development': on the one hand, an absolute monarch, a police state, a primitive agricultural system, an impoverished peasantry, a weak native bourgeoisie; on the other, a technologically advanced industrial sector of giant factories, and a concentrated, combative, politicised working class. The Bolsheviks appreciated some of the implications. Only the proletariat had the potential to lead the revolution. Only mass strikes in the cities could detonate peasant revolt. Only then would the army mutiny and the Tsarist state disintegrate. But there they had stopped. It was Trotsky –

25.   The main exception to this generalisation is the role played in the early development of Trotsky's thinking by Alexander Israel Helphand (aka Parvus). Trotsky met Parvus, a Russian Jewish exile 12 years his senior, in Munich in 1904. He later attributed to Parvus 'the lion's share' of the thinking behind his own theory of permanent revolution. See Cliff 1989, 80–7.

not at the time a Bolshevik (he joined the faction only in the summer of 1917) – who saw further.

To complete and consolidate the victory of democracy over autocracy – to prevent the forces of reaction regrouping to crush the revolution – the proletariat would have to establish a workers' state. Any such state, being class-based, could not be other than an organ of proletarian interests – supporting workers' control of the factories, peasant control of the land, and the dispossession of the rich. Anything less, indeed, would compromise the victory, for it would leave property and power in the hands of class enemies, and, by limiting their gains, would undermine the willingness of the workers and peasants to defend the revolution.[26] Thus, to Lenin's formulation of 'the democratic dictatorship of the proletariat and the peasantry', Trotsky counterposed 'the dictatorship of the proletariat'. In opposition to the schematic conception of two revolutions, different in character, separate in time, he envisaged 'permanent revolution' – that is, a revolution that would not stop part-way, but would instead spill across Russia's borders to the rest of Europe, and would, at the same time, create a popular mass movement of such power that it would strike down all forms of class privilege and inaugurate a new democratic-egalitarian social order. Trotsky's argument, in short, was that a Russian democratic revolution would inevitably 'grow over' into an international socialist revolution.[27]

The proletariat

In ascribing such primacy to the working class, the theory of permanent revolution was making an exceptionally bold

---

26. Cliff 1989, 126–31.
27. Cliff 1989, 80–7, 123–39.

claim. Despite record industrial growth rates since 1890, the Russian proletariat remained relatively small. Trotsky's own estimate was that it comprised about a sixth of the population by 1914, up to 25 million people in all, but that most of these were either village-based rural poor or wage-labourers in small businesses in minor towns, often living and working in their employer's house. The core proletariat – workers in large urban enterprises – numbered only about 3.5 million. Two-thirds of the industrial workers, moreover, were located in just three regions, St Petersburg, Moscow, and the Ukraine. Many of these were new arrivals. The composition of the proletariat reflected rapid industrialisation: many workers were young, many were women, and many retained strong links with the countryside from which they had recently migrated.[28]

Exploitation in the new factories was extreme, and conditions in the fast-expanding industrial quarters appalling. Wages were usually insufficient to support a family. Twelve hour days were common. The accident rate was 11 per cent per year in the mines, 4 per cent in the factories. Discipline was maintained by fines and even corporal punishment.

Aleksei Badayev, one of six Bolsheviks elected to the Duma, the Tsarist parliament, in 1912, reports numerous abuses. On 12 March 1914, for example, he was called to the Treugolnik plant in St Petersburg, where 13,000 mainly women workers were employed making rubber galoshes. They worked a ten-hour day, without a dinner break, some for as little as 40 kopeks, the price of a loaf of black bread. The owners were making 10 million roubles in profit a year.

---

28. Trotsky, 1932–3/1977, 33–4, 55; Kochan 1967/1970, 35–6.

That morning, a new polish had been issued for galoshes ... which emitted poisonous gases. Shortly afterwards, scores of women began to faint. Terrible scenes followed: in some cases the poisoning was so strong that the victims became insane, while in others blood ran from the nose and mouth. The small, badly equipped first-aid room was packed with bodies, and fresh cases were taken into the dining-room, while all who were able to move were sent out of the factory. 'If they drop down there, the police will pick them up' – so ran the cynical excuse of the management.[29]

Housing in the workers' districts was equally stygian. The Baku oil-workers, for instance, were herded into barracks of such squalor that it was, according to one of the bosses, impossible 'without horror and trembling' to pass by them. 'The workers, all in greasy, soot-covered rags, covered with a thick layer of grime and dust, swarm like bees in the extremely dirty and congested quarters. A repulsive smell hits you as soon as you try to approach the window.'

The St Petersburg and Moscow workers generally lived in suburban tenements, but these were no less monstrous. The following is typical of municipal reports at the time:

The apartment has a terrible appearance, the plaster is crumbling, there are holes in the walls, stopped up with rags. It is dirty. The stove has collapsed. Legions of cockroaches and bugs. No double window-frames and so it is piercingly cold. The lavatory is so dilapidated that it is dangerous to

29.   Reed 1926/1977, 274; Badayev 1929/1987, 143–4.

enter and children are not allowed in. All the apartments in the house are similar.[30]

Russia's rulers, eager to catch up industrially with the Western powers, made a virtue of the people's poverty. 'The Russian peasant is much less demanding than the Western European or more particularly the North American worker,' proclaimed Witte, 'and a low wage for Russian enterprise is a fortunate boon, which complements the riches of Russian natural resources.'[31]

But matters were not so simple. Uprooted from the countryside and plunged into a satanic process of break-neck capital accumulation, Russia's young workers fought back in successive waves of mass strikes, each mixing economic struggle and political protest, each stronger and more threatening than the last – the first in the late 1870s, the second in 1896–7, the third in 1903–6, a fourth beginning in 1912. Each time, the workers were hit by savage repression, and each time they learned lessons – about the bosses, the police, and the narks, about unity and solidarity, about whom they could trust in their own ranks, about how to organise and fight. Above all, they learned that economics and politics were inseparable: that when one fought the boss for a living wage, one faced the truncheons and sabres of the Tsarist state. So the fight in the workplaces turned the more determined of the proletarian militants into political revolutionaries – creating a new kind of Russian 'intelligentsia': one formed of self-taught 'worker-intellectuals'.

---

30.   Kochan 1967/1970, 37–9.
31.   Kochan 1967/1970, 40.

The old radical intelligentsia – recruited from the educated elite – had peeled away from the underground movement after 1905. Lenin sneered that nine-tenths of them, perhaps as many as 99 per cent, had gone off to become millionaires, get a cushy office job, or make money in some sort of swindling. 'Young Russian workers', he wrote later, 'now constitute nine-tenths of the organised Marxists in Russia.'[32] This was the general view. Alexander Shlyapnikov, himself a worker-intellectual as well as a leading underground organiser, put it thus: 'The place of the petty-bourgeois intellectuals and student youth was taken up by the intellectual proletarian with calloused hands and highly developed head who had not lost contact with the masses.'[33] Leaflets, newspapers, and pamphlets – smuggled in and circulating illegally – would be read out in small clandestine gatherings and then passed on until they were in tatters and dropped to pieces. Such was the thirst for radical ideas that the underground struggled to satisfy it, especially in the war years, under intensified police repression. 'The demand for illegal socialist literature', recalled Shlyapnikov,

> was so great that the poor illegal technology could not meet it. Private initiative came to its aid. Every sort of manuscript, hectographed or retyped copy of individual proclamations, articles from illegal publications abroad, etc., circulated among the workers. A typewritten copy of Lenin and Zinoviev's *The War and Socialism* [a pamphlet] was passed from hand to hand around Moscow. *Social Democrat* and *Communist* [newspapers] were such luxuries that 50 kopeks or a rouble would be paid for one reading. There were

32. Cliff 1975/1986, 353–4.
33. Le Blanc 1993/2015, 171–2.

demands for hundreds of copies of *Communist*, and workers
would readily put aside three roubles of pay for a copy.

When the underground printing presses could not produce
enough, 'enthusiastic amateurs existed who would copy out
whole pamphlets by hand'.[34]

Much nonsense has been written about Lenin and the
Bolsheviks. He has been caricatured as a ruthless and
manipulative authoritarian, his followers as the cult-like dupes
of a man set upon personal dictatorship and fulfilment of
a messianic mission. Thus, the argument runs, the roots of
Stalin's Gulags are to be found in the 'democratic centralism'
of Lenin's party. The caricature has many facets. One is the
claim that Lenin set out to build – and succeeded in building
– a party in which middle-class intellectuals presided over
working-class foot soldiers. The opposite is true: the Bolshevik
Party of 1912–17 – the largely new party that emerged as the
Russian labour movement recovered from the defeat of 1905
– was, both by intention and in actuality, overwhelmingly
working class in composition and thoroughly democratic
in nature. What *is* true is that the building of that party was
first and foremost the achievement of Lenin. And because his
achievement is so contested and misconstrued, we must give
the rise of the Bolsheviks – the party that made the revolution
– detailed attention.

---

34. Shlyapnikov 1923/1982, 92, 156.

CHAPTER THREE

Lenin and the Bolsheviks

Lenin's *Iskra*. Underground revolutionary propaganda
ate like an acid into the social fabric of Old Russia.

Early on the morning of 5 May 1887, a small steamer delivered five students, shackled in irons, to the Schlusselburg Fortress on the River Neva, a short distance from St Petersburg. They were held in separate cells, small and whitewashed, with stone floors and iron doors, for three days. Then, on 8 May, they were woken in the early hours and led into the prison courtyard, where three wooden scaffolds had been erected. They were hanged in two batches. Two of them, before they died, cried out the name of their party: 'Long live *Narodnya Volya*!'

They had been condemned to death for membership of a 'criminal society attempting to overturn the existing state and social order by means of violent revolution'. They had, the prosecutors explained, organised a 'secret circle for terrorist activity' and were planning to assassinate Tsar Alexander III.

One of the five was called Alexander Ulyanov.[1] The 20-year-old son of a school inspector and minor notable, he had been brought up in Simbirsk, a dull provincial town on the River Volga. His younger brother was still attending high school there. His name was Vladimir Ilyich Ulyanov. The world would come to know him as 'Lenin'.

The man who became the leader of the Bolsheviks is incomprehensible without his Narodnik background. The young radicals of *Narodnya Volya* were the heroes of Lenin's youth. Though he never spoke of his brother in public, there can be little doubt that Alexander's martyrdom affected him deeply. He read and re-read *What is to be Done?*, and his private photo albums contained several pictures of Chernyshevsky. His wife and comrade, Nadezhda Krupskaya, tells us that he always held 'the old revolutionaries of the *Narodnya Volya* in great

---

1. Salisbury 1977/1978, 1–4.

respect'.[2] At the end of his own *What is to be Done?* (1902) – so-named, of course, in honour of Chernyshevsky – he wrote of Russia's new generation of revolutionaries as follows:

Nearly all of them in their early youth enthusiastically worshipped the terrorist heroes. It was a great wrench to abandon the captivating impressions of these heroic traditions, and it was accompanied by the breaking off of personal relationships with people who were determined to remain loyal to *Narodnya Volya* and for whom the young Social Democrats had profound respect.[3]

This was autobiography: this was the difficult journey taken by the man whose brother had swung in the noose of a Tsarist hangman for his allegiance to *Narodnya Volya*.

The Narodniks failed because they attempted to substitute the individual terrorism of revolutionaries for the collective action of the masses. Lenin and his followers were inspired by the romantic heroism of the Narodniks, but appalled by the futility and waste. They understood – even admired – the impatience and idealism, but at the same time knew that history could not be forced. The essence of Lenin's politics – worked out between 1888, when he first read Marx, and 1902, when he wrote *What is to be Done?* – was to think of revolution as a process for which an engine had to be constructed. His design had four main parts. These were: a vision of the world transformed by revolutionary action; an underground activist network to turn this vision into a framework political organisation; the growing of this organisation into a mass

2. Krupskaya 1960/1975, 40, 47–8, 82–3; Lih 2011, 19–31.

3. Lenin 1902, 189.

social movement through recruitment of the most militant people in every industrial centre; and the eventual role of this essentially proletarian-urban movement in detonating a country-wide insurrection of the Russian *Narod*. Let us consider this 'blueprint' for revolution in more detail.

The concept of revolution

Marxism can be defined as the theory and practice of international working-class revolution. When the young revolutionaries Karl Marx and Frederick Engels were first working out their ideas in the early 1840s, they confronted what appeared to be a historical riddle. The steady rise in the productivity of human labour throughout history meant increasing capacity to abolish want. Yet a minority continued to enjoy grotesque wealth while millions lived in poverty. The riddle was: who might so reorder the world that human labour served human need?

Their answer to this question was the new working class – or proletariat – being created by the Industrial Revolution. This was partly because it was an exploited class, one with no vested interest in the system, with, as they put it, 'nothing to lose but its chains'. But this had been true of the slaves of ancient Rome and the serfs of medieval Europe. A second factor was decisive. The workers – unlike slaves or peasants – could not emancipate themselves through *individual* appropriation of private property. They were part of a complex international division of labour, such that only *collective* control over the means of production, distribution, and exchange could provide a credible alternative to capitalism. The village might march on the mansion, evict the landlord, and divide up the estate into small plots. The situation of the workers was quite different. Concentrated in factories and cities, the workers were bound to act collectively. And, since they could not partition a textile mill, railway line, or telegraph network, were they to take power as a class, they would be obliged to rule collectively. The proletariat was therefore the first class in history with a *general interest in the emancipation of humanity as a whole*.

The 1848 Revolutions – which swept across Europe that year, with armed uprisings in Paris, Berlin, Vienna, Budapest, Prague, Rome, and a dozen other major cities – led Marx and Engels to another radical conclusion: that the proletariat was the only class capable of *any* sort of determined revolutionary action. During the armed uprisings, the liberal bourgeoisie, fearful of social upheaval, had stood paralysed as the cannon of counter-revolution cleared the barricade-fighters from the streets. 'In the best of cases,' Engels later wrote, 'the bourgeoisie is an unheroic class. Even its most brilliant victories – in England in the 17th century or in France in the 18th – had not been won by it itself, but had been won for it by the plebeian masses of people.' This was quite so. Without action from below by revolutionary crowds in London, and later by the soldiers of the New Model Army, the English Revolution would have stalled. Equally, without repeat insurrections by the Parisian *sansculottes* – in 1789, 1792, and 1793 – the Jacobins, the most resolute of the French bourgeois revolutionaries, would never have come to power. But the German bourgeoisie of 1848 seemed to have plumbed new depths of 'stupidity and cowardice', and the searing experience of its spinelessness, culminating in a comprehensive defeat for democracy, had compelled Marx and Engels to reconfigure their conception of what they – like Trotsky much later – called 'permanent revolution'.[4]

This represented an extraordinary shift of perspective and strategy. Marx was, in effect, announcing that the bourgeois revolution was over, that the struggle for democratic reform was now inextricably bound up with that for social reform, and that henceforward the sole agent of revolution was the (at that time still embryonic) industrial proletariat. He, and to a greater extent Engels, later retreated from the radicalism of this conception (of 1849), and there seems to be little trace of it in late nineteenth-century Marxism. The Russian Social Democrats were therefore confused about the nature of their own imminent revolution – confused to the point of bitter controversy.

Lenin's position (until 1917) was that of the mainstream – but with a Russian twist. He argued that revolutionary action by the proletariat and peasantry was necessary to accomplish the tasks of the 'bourgeois revolution' – the overthrow of the autocracy, the establishment of a democratic republic, a redistribution of land to the peasants, and an eight-hour day in the factories. The autocracy would not relinquish power voluntarily, therefore revolution was necessary. But the liberal bourgeoisie was bound to betray the revolution, so that 'the only force capable of gaining a decisive victory over Tsarism is the people, i.e. the proletariat and the peasantry ... The revolution's decisive victory over Tsarism means the establishment of the revolutionary-democratic dictatorship of the proletariat and the peasantry.'[5]

---

4.   Draper 1978, 201–49, 268.
5.   Cliff 1975/1986, 198.

What the Marxist philosopher Georg Lukács called 'the actuality of the revolution' was at the very core of Lenin's politics. He was, on his Russian side, a descendant of the Decembrists and Narodniks, and on his European, of Marx and Engels. In him, the romantic tradition of revolutionary heroes battling a police state was allied to the theory and practice of international working-class revolution. More precisely – and true to Marx's axiom that 'the emancipation of the working class will be the act of the working class' – the two conceptions fused in Leninism, such that the heroic leader of the people became the revolutionary proletariat itself.[6]

Lenin's touchstone became the revolutionary programme adopted by the Russian Social Democratic Labour Party at its Second Congress in 1903. Written by Plekhanov and effectively the party's founding statement, Lenin, for the rest of his political career, would insist upon adherence to it – in opposition to backsliders and renegades – as the true measure of socialist commitment. It was unequivocal:

the Russian Social Democratic Labour Party takes as its most immediate political task the overthrow of the Tsarist autocracy and its replacement by a democratic republic … In striving to achieve its immediate aims, the RSDLP supports every oppositional and revolutionary movement directed against the social and political order prevailing in Russia … the RSDLP is firmly convinced that complete, consistent, and lasting realisation of … [radical change] … is attainable only through the overthrow of the autocracy

6. Lukács 1924/1970/2009, 9–13 and passim; Lih 2011, 14–15 and passim.

and the convocation of a constituent assembly, freely elected by the entire people.[7]

The revolutionary underground

Radical ideas, if they are to become an historical force, must be turned into political organisation. A vision of the world transformed is pie in the sky without a revolutionary party. On the other hand, there is no blueprint for revolutionary parties. History reveals many different kinds. It also shows them forming, growing, and changing as organic parts of mass movements. The Levellers, the Chartists, the Jacobins, and the Communards can all be regarded as alternative forms of revolutionary party. The Bolshevik faction of the Russian Social Democratic Labour Party was yet another kind. What all of these have in common is a) that they were mass parties rooted in social movements, and b) that they developed organically over time. The Bolshevik leader Grigori Zinoviev explained that a party

is a living organism connected by millions of threads with the class from which it emerges. A party takes shape over years and even decades … the living dialectical formation of a party is a very complex, lengthy, and difficult process. It is born amid sharp pangs, and it is subject to perpetual crystallisations, regroupings, splits, and trials in the heat of struggle before it finally takes shape as a party of the proletariat … [8]

A revolutionary party, then, is not a thing that springs ready-made into existence – like Athena from the head of

---

7.   Plekhanov 1904/1978, 6, 9.

8.   Zinoviev 1923/1973, 12–13.

Zeus at the stroke of history's hammer – but is something that evolves continuously in an organic relationship with the class movement of which it is part. The revolutionary party is never in a state of *being*, only ever in a state of *becoming*.[9]

So it was with the Bolsheviks. The 'prehistory' of Russian Social Democracy can be traced back to the establishment of a 'Chaikovist' group in St Petersburg in 1870, a 'South Russian Workers' League' in Odessa in 1875, and a 'North Russian Workers' League' in St Petersburg in 1878. All these organisations, however, were tiny, short-lived, and intellectually inchoate. More substantial – and explicitly Marxist – was the 'Emancipation of Labour Group' formed by Georgi Plekhanov in St Petersburg in 1883, after he and a handful of other intellectuals had made the break with Narodnik populism and committed themselves to building a proletarian party.

But the impact of Russia's socialist pioneers was minimal. Though the state-driven industrialisation programme was gathering steam, the working class remained relatively small. There had been a miniature strike wave in the late 1870s, but severe repression following the assassination of the Tsar in 1881 smothered both incipient labour militancy and embryonic socialist organisation for a decade. Russian Social Democrats could be numbered in the tens, most of them exiles. Plekhanov remained their standard-bearer. 'The Russian revolution will either triumph as a revolution of the working class,' he declared at the First Congress of the Second International in 1889, 'or it will not triumph at all.'[10]

There are desert plants that lie dormant for years only to erupt suddenly into life when finally it rains. Plekhanov's big

---

9.   Lukács 1924/1970/2009, 37.

10.   Zinoviev 1923/1973, 18–37 passim; Cliff 1975/1986, 21–7 passim.

idea was of this kind. It was a seed hidden in the social depths awaiting an eruption of mass struggle that would allow it to burst forth. It was a long time coming, but then, in the mid 1890s, Russia's new industrial districts were rocked by strikes far bigger than those of the late 1870s. A new generation of revolutionary intellectuals – including a young Lenin, who had arrived in the capital from provincial Simbirsk two years previously – were active supporters of the strikes. In 1895, Lenin and others founded the St Petersburg League of Struggle for the Emancipation of the Working Class. The movement peaked in May 1896 with a three-week strike by 30,000 St Petersburg textile workers in which the League of Struggle played a leading organisational role. Russian Social Democracy thus became a small mass movement. Its committed activists were now to be numbered in the hundreds.

But the movement subsided. Lenin and five other members of the St Petersburg League had been arrested in December 1895 and sentenced to terms of exile in Siberia. When the remnants of several groups met in Minsk in March 1898, this 'First Congress' of Russian Social Democrats comprised just nine delegates. No party programme was adopted, and eight of the delegates, including two of the three newly elected Central Committee members, were arrested within days.[11]

Lenin, meantime, had three years of exile to reflect on his experience of the class struggle and the socialist underground. When he returned to active politics in 1899, he had a fully worked out strategy for building a revolutionary party in Russia. Much of the debate about 'Leninism' hinges on inter-pretations of Lenin's theory and practice in this crucial period,

11. Zinoviev 1923/1973, 47–53 passim; Cliff 1975/1986, 42–68 passim.

between 1899 and 1903, when 'Bolshevism' emerged as a distinct current within Russian Social Democracy.

Despite much ill-informed commentary to the contrary – by both enthusiasts and detractors – Lenin's Bolshevik Party was never a 'democratic-centralist' sect. A political sect can be defined as a small organisation run by a self-appointed 'vanguard' that seeks to insert itself into a mass movement in order to grow parasitically like a tic. A 'democratic-centralist' organisation is one where power is concentrated in the hands of a (largely) self-perpetuating leadership, or even in the hands of a single cult-like guru. Small organisations of this kind exist in all periods. Mass revolutionary parties, on other hand, are never like this. The reason is simple: revolution 'from below' – that is, revolution where the emancipation of the masses is the act of the masses themselves – means an explosion of democracy. Here is how Trotsky described it in his *History of the Russian Revolution*:

> The most indubitable feature of a revolution is the direct interference of the masses in historic events … at those crucial moments when the old order becomes no longer endurable to the masses, they break over the barriers excluding them from the political arena, sweep aside their traditional representatives, and create by their own interference the initial groundwork for a new regime … This history of a revolution is for us first of all a history of the forcible entrance of the masses into the realm of rulership over their own destiny.[12]

---

12. Trotsky 1932–3/1977, 17.

The ideal to which Lenin and the Bolsheviks aspired was therefore an open, mass, democratic party capable of giving effective expression to the revolutionary energy of the Russian working class. Their model was the German Social Democratic Party (SPD). The largest working-class organisation in the world, and the dominant force in the Second International (a confederation of European socialist parties), by 1912 the SPD had a million members, was publishing 90 daily papers, and ran a women's section, a youth section, various trade unions and co-ops, and numerous sports clubs and cultural societies. In that year, it made a dramatic electoral breakthrough, winning one in three votes, becoming, with 110 seats, the largest party in the Reichstag, the German parliament. In the space of a generation, it had been transformed from a small outlawed minority into a mass social movement and electoral machine.[13] The SPD's theoretical foundation-stone was Karl Kautsky's *Erfurt Programme* (1892), a book-length treatise on the perspective and strategy of the up-and-coming German workers' party. That Lenin translated it into Russian in 1894 tells us everything we need to know about his political debt to Kautsky and the SPD.[14] That this debt was huge is confirmed by the testimony of other Bolsheviks, all of whom, without apparent exception, regarded the SPD as a model socialist party.[15]

---

13. Faulkner 2013, 186–7.

14. Lih 2011, 42–3 and passim; here, and on a much grander scale in Lih 2008/2013, Lars Lih sets out a compelling case that Lenin, so far from being a 'democratic-centralist' setting out to create 'a party of a new type', was in fact a mainstream European Social Democrat, at least up until 1914, and to some degree until as late as 1917.

15. Shlyapnikov 1923/1982, 16–17.

The problem in Russia was the police. How do you build a mass democratic party in a police state? To organise openly was impossible, and without open organisation you could neither make democratic decisions nor hold democratic elections. Indeed, the looser the network, the more vulnerable it was to penetration by the police. The more people you had attending a meeting, especially when many were new and inexperienced in underground work, the greater the risk of discovery and arrests. How, in these circumstances, could the party make democratic decisions? How could the leadership be democratically chosen? The simple fact was that democracy and police repression were polar opposites. Two questions therefore imposed themselves on Russia's Social Democratic underground: a) how best to build socialist organisation in Tsarist Russia; and b) how best to uphold the principles and programme of the party.

'The closer the end of our exile drew in sight,' wrote Krupskaya, Lenin's partner,

the more did Vladimir Ilyich think about the work facing us. The news from Russia was scanty. 'Economism' was gaining ground there, and there was no party to speak of. We had no printing plants in Russia ... Party work was completely disorganised, and constant arrests made any continuity impossible.[16]

'Economism' was a reformist argument inside Russian Social Democracy to the effect that the workers should concern themselves with the 'economic' struggle for improved conditions and leave the 'political' struggle for democracy

16. Krupskaya 1960/1975, 44.

to the liberals. It reflected a mechanical view of the coming Russian revolution as 'bourgeois' rather than 'proletarian'.[17] That this idea could gain so much traction among Russian socialists was, for Lenin, a symptom of the organisational and ideological disintegration of the party.

Lenin's plan for the reconstruction of Social Democracy was two-fold. First, he proposed the publication of an all-Russian socialist newspaper. This would be produced abroad, smuggled into Russia, and then distributed to the underground groups across the country. A coherent set of revolutionary-socialist ideas disseminated in this way would cement together the party's activist network and help it recruit new members. Moreover, the very process of illegal distribution would itself create and sustain the network. 'A paper is what we need above all', he wrote.

> Without it we cannot systematically carry on that extensive and theoretically sound propaganda and agitation which is the principal and constant duty of the Social Democrats ... Our movement, intellectually as well as practically (organisationally), suffers most of all from being scattered, from the fact that the vast majority of Social Democrats are almost entirely immersed in local work, which narrows their point-of-view, limits their activities, and affects their conspiratorial skill and training ... The Russian working class ... betrays a constant desire for political knowledge – they demand illegal literature, not only during periods of unusual unrest, but at all times.

---

17.   Cliff 1975/1986, 59–66.

Political education was one function of the revolutionary paper. There was another. He continued:

> the role of the paper is not confined solely to the spreading of ideas, to political education, and to procuring allies. A paper is not merely a collective propagandist and collective agitator; it is also a collective organiser. In that respect, it can be compared to the scaffolding erected around a building in construction ... With the aid of, and around, a paper, there will automatically develop an organisation ... The mere technical problem of procuring a regular supply of material for the newspaper and its regular distribution will make it necessary to create a network of agents of a united party ... This network of agents will form the skeleton of the organisation we need.[18]

The second part of Lenin's plan was to tighten party organisation to make it more impervious to police penetration. This is perhaps the most widely misconstrued aspect of Lenin's work. An immediate practical response to the problem posed by the Tsarist police has been elevated into either a universal principle of revolutionary organisation (in the case of sectarians) or into a grand strategy for the construction of a totalitarian dictatorship (among right-wing commentators). Here is what Lenin actually proposed:

> The leadership of the movement should be entrusted to the smallest possible number of the most homogeneous possible groups of professional revolutionaries with great practical experience. Participation in the movement would

---

18.   Lenin 1901, 112–15.

extend to the greatest possible number of the most diverse and heterogeneous groups of the most varied sections of the proletariat (and other classes of the people) ... We must centralise the leadership of the movement. We must also ... as far as possible decentralise responsibility to the party on the part of its individual members, of every participant in its work, and of every circle belonging to or associated with the party. This decentralisation is an essential prerequisite of revolutionary centralisation and an essential corrective to it.[19]

This can be summarised as: keep the core cells of the party centralised and closed (to protect them from the police); but encourage the highest possible level of initiative and activity on the part of the wider mass movement within which the party is embedded.

The first all-Russian socialist newspaper – *Iskra* ('The Spark') – was launched in December 1900. Over the next three years, while Lenin was on the editorial board (he was destined to lose control of his own creation), a total of 51 issues appeared.[20] The establishment of *Iskra* was uncontroversial, but the other part of Lenin's plan – to make the party more police-resistant – proved far more problematic: it was, in fact, the origin of a factional dispute that would divide the party for more than a decade.

It blew up – unexpectedly – at the Second Congress of the RSDLP (the first proper conference), held in Brussels and London in July-August 1903. About 60 people attended (though not all with voting rights) and virtually all the

19.   Cliff 1975/1986, 91–2.
20.   Lih 2011, 73–5.

major industrial cities and regions were represented.[21] Lenin worked hard in preparing the conference, hoping to match the achievement of founding *Iskra* with the creation of 'a united solid party, merging into one all the detached groups ... a party in which there would be no artificial barriers' (Krupskaya).[22] He set out his vision in advance in a long pamphlet destined to become one of his most famous publications: *What is to be Done?* It ends with this rallying cry to all the revolutionary forces of Russia:

> If we genuinely succeed in getting all or a significant majority of local committees, local groups, and circles actively to take up the common work, we would in short order be able to have a weekly newspaper, regularly distributed in tens of thousands of copies throughout Russia. This newspaper would be a small part of a huge bellows that blows up each flame of class struggle and popular indignation into a common fire. Around this task ... an army of experienced fighters would systematically be recruited and trained. Among the ladders and scaffolding of this common organisational construction would soon rise up Social Democratic Zheliabovs from among our revolutionaries, Russian Bebels from our workers, who would be pushed forward and then take their place at the head of a mobilised army and would raise up the whole *Narod* to settle accounts with the shame and curse of Russia.[23]

---

21.   Zinoviev 1923/1973, 84–5.
22.   Krupskaya 1960/1975, 85.
23.   Lih 2011, 82–3.

This passage encapsulates the fusion of theoretical clarity, practical measures, and revolutionary romanticism that was the essence of Lenin's politics – in contrast to the desiccated conceptions of both sectarians and reactionaries. The newspaper will create and bind together an underground network. The network will combine the heroism of Narodniks (like Zheliabov) with the politics of Social Democrats (like the German SPD leader Bebel). It will fan into flame a movement of the whole people (the *Narod*: workers and peasants) powerful enough to destroy the Tsarist regime.[24]

For some, the vision was an inspirational dream. For others, it was a nightmare. Though issues became tangled and allegiances shifted, in the succession of rows that divided the Second Congress can be detected a fundamental difference between those who sought compromises with others and those whose aim was proletarian revolution.

The most significant argument arose over a seemingly minor issue: the definition of a party member. Lenin proposed that the statutes should define a member as one 'who recognises the party's programme and supports it by material means *and by personal participation in one of the party organisations*'. Martov proposed deleting the final phrase and replacing it with '*and by regular personal association under the direction of one of the party organisations*'.[25] The issue at stake was simple: was the party to be formed only of the activist vanguard, or was it to include anyone loosely 'associated' with the party?

There was nothing elitist about Lenin's conception: anyone could choose to become a party activist. His point was that *only* those who committed themselves in this way should be

24. Lih 2011, 82.
25. RSDLP 1904/1978, 320–34; Cliff 1975/1986, 108–10.

empowered to make decisions. The risk otherwise was that the politics of the party would be diluted by a lukewarm swamp of passive 'members'. At root, Lenin argued, Martov was confusing party and class:

> the party must be only the vanguard, the leader of the vast masses of the working class, the whole (or nearly the whole) of which works 'under the control and direction' of the party organisations, but the whole of which does not and should not belong to a 'party' ... when our activities have to be confined to limited, secret circles and even to private meetings, it is extremely difficult, almost impossible in fact, for us to distinguish those who only talk from those who do the work ... It would be better if ten who do work should not call themselves party members ... than that one who only talks should have the right and opportunity to be a party member.[26]

Lenin was right. The revolutionaries were a minority swimming against the current. Confronting them was the whole power of official society, which, by force and by fraud, was deployed to contain the class struggle. When the workers came onto the streets, they faced force – the batons and bullets of the police. The rest of the time, they were sold a fraud – that God had ordained the social order, that the Tsar was their 'Little Father', that the Jews were the enemy. Most workers, in consequence, had a 'mixed consciousness'. Because they were victims of the system, they were open to the arguments of revolutionaries, especially in moments when they gained confidence through collective struggle. But because they were

26. Cliff 1975/1986, 108–9.

also ground down by the system, they were rarely wholly free of what Marx called 'the muck of ages' – the piety, deference, and racism that conspire to keep people in their place by their own decision.

If this were not the case – if the working class was instinctively and spontaneously revolutionary – there would be no need for a party. Martov's conception, where the party is dissolved into the mass, would then be the right one. But in reality class consciousness is contested and contradictory. A battle of ideas rages across society, with socialists on one side and the propagandists of the system on the other. Consciousness is therefore uneven across the working class. Because of this, the party must comprise a vanguard of worker-activists who have broken decisively with the old order, who reject all its reactionary arguments, who embrace the vision of a world transformed, who come, individually and collectively, to embody 'the actuality of the revolution'. Only a party so formed would be capable of resisting the pull to the right – towards what was called, in the political discourse of the time, 'conciliationism' or 'liquidationism' – and instead constitute a solid pole of attraction for the accumulation of revolutionary forces.

A line was drawn at the Second Congress between reformists, henceforward known as 'Mensheviks' (meaning 'supporters of the minority'), and revolutionaries, henceforward 'Bolsheviks' ('supporters of the majority'). Lenin lost some votes, won others, and emerged in control of the party leadership. But he later found himself displaced as allegiances shifted again inside the small groups of Russian political exiles whose self-appointed task it was to sustain the party infrastructure and supply it with literature. He fretted over the divisions, doubted their significance, made overtures to repair relationships. It seemed absurd, with so much at stake, with such a sound plan in place, that the party should be wrecked by faction.

The divisions, however, were real. Time would show this. The mass of RSDLP members favoured unity. The workers were intolerant of squabbles among exiled party intellectuals, who appeared self-indulgent and irresponsible to those engaged in day-to-day struggle against the bosses and the police. Partly because of this, relations between the two factions see-sawed between split and semi-unity until January 1912, when, at a small party congress in Prague convened by the Bolsheviks but boycotted by the Mensheviks, Lenin's followers assumed authority over the RSDLP.[27] What made this event decisive was that the Bolsheviks now enjoyed an overwhelming majority among the activists of the revolutionary underground inside Russia, and that the working-class movement in which they were embedded was entering upon a new phase of mass struggle.

So the division in the RSDLP was not a sudden event engineered by a dogmatic 'splitter' in 1903; it was a decade-long process in which a powerful instinct for unity was eventually overwhelmed by intractable differences. Nor was the substantive issue – as the common caricature would have it – Bolshevik 'centralism' versus Menshevik 'democracy'. As soon as police repression was lifted and open party-building became possible – as during the 1905 Revolution – Lenin starting denouncing the centralism and conservatism of Social Democratic activists. 'We need young forces', he wrote in February 1905:

---

27.   Le Blanc 1993/2015, 159–66.

I am for shooting on the spot anyone who presumes to say that there are no people to be had. The people in Russia are legion; all we have to do is to recruit young people more widely and boldly ... without fearing them. This is a time of war. The youth – students, and still more so the young workers – will decide the issue of the struggle. Get rid of all the old habits of immobility, of respect for rank, and so on. Form hundreds of [party] circles ... from among the youth and encourage them to work full blast ... Allow every sub-committee to write and publish leaflets without any red tape (there is no harm if they do make a mistake) ... Do not fear their lack of training, do not tremble at their inexperience and lack of development ... Only you must be sure to organise, organise, and organise hundreds of circles, completely pushing into the background the customary, well-meant committee (hierarchic) stupidities.[28]

Lenin's problem in 1905 was the inherent conservatism of all human organisation. Without a degree of routine and continuity, no stable political party can exist. But when the tide turns, the party must go with it or be left washed up on the beach. The 'professional revolutionaries' of 1903 – the *Comitetchiki* (committee-people) – became barriers to the creation of a mass democratic party in 1905. They feared 'dilution' of the party. Lenin railed against them, demanding mass recruitment of young workers and the replacement of intellectuals by workers on party bodies. 'The inertness of the committee-people has to be overcome', he proclaimed. 'Workers have the class instinct, and, given some political experience, they pretty soon become staunch Social

28.   Cliff 1975/1986, 171–2.

Democrats. I should be strongly in favour of having eight workers to every two intellectuals on our committees.'[29]

What is to be Done? and the 1903 split have become fetishised – transformed into the holy text and founding ritual of a mythological 'party of a new type'. The truth is that Lenin was 'a man of the people' to his inner core; that all his political instincts were deeply democratic; and that his politics were rooted in a profound belief in the transformative power of mass working-class action. Everything else was secondary: a matter of the strategy and tactics necessary to unleash the torrential force of a democracy shackled by a police state. As Krupskaya explained it, reflecting on Lenin's early years as a propagandist and agitator among the St Petersburg workers:

Vladimir Ilyich had implicit faith in the proletariat's class instinct, its creative powers, and historic mission. This faith had not come suddenly to Vladimir Ilyich, but had been hammered out during the years when he had studied and pondered Marx's theory of the class struggle, when he had studied Russian realities, and learnt, in fighting the ideas of the old revolutionaries [the Narodniks], to offset the heroism of the solitary fighter by the strength and heroism of the class struggle. It was not just blind faith in an unknown force, but a deep-rooted belief in the strength of the proletariat and its tremendous role in the cause of working-class emancipation, a belief founded on a profound knowledge and thorough study of the facts of life. His work among the St Petersburg proletariat had helped to

29.   Cliff 1975/1986, 174.

identify this faith in the power of the working class with real live people.[30]

The activist vanguard

Osip Piatnitsky was an active socialist for more than 40 years. A Polish Jew and apprentice tailor, he was introduced to Social Democratic politics by his two older brothers and his workmates at the age of 14. He was soon active in the illegal tailors' union, in the *Bund*, the Jewish socialist party affiliated to the RSDLP, and in a clandestine political discussion circle (the boundaries between union, party, and circle were highly porous in the underground movement). Experience of strikes and street clashes with Cossacks and police hardened his politics. In the winter of 1900/1, he broke with the *Bund* in opposition to its Jewish separatism, becoming an '*Iskra*-ist', a member of the group that would soon evolve into the Bolsheviks. Despite awesome personal sacrifice – periods of unemployment, poverty, homelessness, and hunger; periods of imprisonment and Siberian exile – his will remained unbroken.[31] He was an archetypal 'worker-Bolshevik', a 'professional revolutionary' in the manner of Lenin's *What is to be Done?*, the kind who, in Trotsky's description, 'dedicates himself completely to the labour movement under conditions of illegality and forced conspiracy'.[32] A rare survivor from the earliest years, he was, like so many of the Old Bolsheviks, eventually murdered by Stalin's police (in 1938).

30. Krupskaya 1960/1975, 108.
31. Piatnitsky 1935, 15–28 and passim.
32. Le Blanc 1993/2015, 14.

How did the revolutionary underground to which Piatnitsky belonged operate? Leaflets might be printed on a secret press, reproduced on a hectograph machine, or even copied out by hand. They would then be distributed in bundles at a clandestine meeting and each activist allocated one or more streets for delivery. Copies of revolutionary pamphlets and newspapers might be smuggled across the Russo-German frontier in Poland or (later) across the Russo-Finnish border in the far north, and from there distributed across Russia in suitcases with false bottoms, in 'breastplates' (coats with literature sewn into the lining), and even in picture-frames and book-covers. Wafer-thin paper was used, and the margins might be cut off to reduce weight further.[33]

Because demand exceeded the supply that could be smuggled, efforts to run illegal print-shops were relentless. The 'Caucasian Fruit Shop' in Moscow's Rozhdestvensky Boulevard, for instance, was the front for a secret printing-press in the basement. The 'shopkeeper' was a party member, and deliveries of printing supplies and dispatches of printed material were boxed as 'Caucasian fruit'. The print-shop, a small room artificially lit, contained an American press, a work-bench, trays of type, and boxes of paper. The thud of the press could be heard in the shop above, so a bell was installed to give warning to stop when a customer entered. Urgent work would be done by two activists working through the night. The press existed for eight months, from September 1906 to April 1907, before being discovered by the police. In this period, 45 separate publications were issued. These included addresses, manifestos, pamphlets, journals, numerous leaflets

---

33.   Piatnitsky 1935, 25, 39, 57–8, 69.

(these with a total print-run of 1.5 million), and a small May Day poster (print-run 350,000).[34]

In this way, the exiled leadership reached deep into the Russian proletarian movement. But success depended upon a painstakingly constructed top-down network. Piatnitsky, appointed Odessa organiser in 1905, explains:

> The organisation of that time, in Odessa as well as in the rest of Russia, was built from top to bottom on the principle of co-optation. In the plants and factories and in the workshops, the Bolsheviks who worked there invited (co-opted) workers whom they considered to be class-conscious and who were devoted to the cause.[35]

On this foundation, through careful selection, was constructed an edifice of district, regional, and city-wide committees.

> City committees had the right to co-opt new members. When a city committee was arrested as a body, the central committee of the party designated one or more members to form a new committee, and those appointed co-opted suitable comrades from the workers of that region to complete the new committee.[36]

There was no other way. The risks were too high. Any open organisation would immediately have been penetrated by informers. Any amateur slip-up could lead the Tsarist police direct to a meeting-place and result in mass arrests.

---

34. Piatnitsky 1935, 107–10, 120–1.

35. Piatnitsky 1935, 76–7.

36. Piatnitsky 1935, 77.

Underground revolutionary work required skill, experience, and exceptional precautions. Prison, torture, even death stalked the movement's activists. Piatnitsky was mortified when one of his collaborators, a foundry worker, was caught with illegal literature:

> They beat Solomon Rogut until he lost consciousness, and dragged him naked from the police station to the police headquarters, demanding the names of his comrades and where he got the literature ... Solomon Rogut was sent to the Kovno prison. A month later, we learned that he had hanged himself (it was never established whether he really committed suicide or was beaten to death) ... it left an indelible impression on me: I had caused the death of a comrade.[37]

For a revolutionary to remain at large in Tsarist Russia was to play an exhausting game of cat-and-mouse with the police. Activists travelled under false names, with made-up identities, carrying forged passports, often wearing disguises. If aware, or suspecting, that they were under surveillance, they would take long detours on the way to a rendezvous, dodging down alleyways and disappearing through tenements and backyards; jumping onto passing tramcars was an especially popular way of getting away from a police tail. More wearisome still was the lack of a home. Activists known to the police might have to change lodgings every few days. Piatnitsky would sometimes find himself trudging the streets or sleeping rough, unable to return to lodgings being watched by the police, unable to find

---

37. Piatnitsky 1935, 32–3.

alternative accommodation. Just to exist as a revolutionary could be a full-time occupation.[38]

Most veterans of the struggle endured periods of imprisonment and exile. The experience was variable. In the Lukyanovskaya prison in Kiev in 1902, the regime was exceptionally relaxed. Piatnitsky found it full of rebellious middle-class students, who had forced major concessions from the governor. On the political wing, where large numbers of *Iskra*-ists were being held, cell doors were open from morning till night, as was the door to the exercise yard, and inmates spent their time reading and debating. 'The prison thus became my university', Piatnitsky recalled. 'I began to read systematically under the guidance of an educated Marxist who knew the revolutionary and Marxist literature very well.'[39]

Twelve years later, however, awaiting dispatch into Siberian exile, the Samara prison was far worse – head shaved, forced to wear prison uniform, no mixing with other politicals, hard labour cleaning cells, solitary confinement for minor offences, strip searches in the bitter cold. After a six-month wait, the passage to Siberia was made partly on foot, sleeping in filthy peasant huts without washing facilities; 'there were biting frosts with snow-storms which made our progress on the snow-covered roads difficult'. The end of the long trek was the benighted wilderness village of Fedino, where the inhabitants slept in their clothing all year round, the beds, walls, and floorboards were infested with bugs and cockroaches, and life was 'unbearably dull'.[40]

38. Piatnitsky 1935, 96, 114, 123–4.

39. Piatnitsky 1935, 36–41.

40. Piatnitsky 1935, 205–20.

Again and again, organisation was destroyed by mass arrests and had to be built anew, the scattered fragments reassembled, new forces recruited to replace those lost to the prisons. Long before the final split with the Mensheviks in 1912, this spider's web, spread across Russia and connected by long threads to the exiled leadership abroad, was Lenin's party. Here, in the revolutionary underground, under the searching gaze of the Tsarist police, there was no place for the half-hearted, the fair-weather friend, the salon intellectual. To operate in the netherworld of illegal activism required high levels of commitment and endurance. The revolutionary paper provided the cohesive. It was, explained Piatnitsky, 'the centre of gravitation for all the heterogeneous revolutionary elements of the Russian working class'; and when Lenin lost control of *Iskra* and was forced to create a new organ – *Vperyod* ('Forward') – the same network distributed it, for 'the transport apparatus in Russia was in the hands of the party majority'. Here, in the lower depths of the social order, the mole of history was at work: one of the secrets of the Bolshevik Revolution is that the activist vanguard of the RSDLP was, from the earliest days, instinctively Leninist.[41]

The effectiveness of this vanguard is incomprehensible if we imagine them to be the cult-like groupies of a remote guru – as the caricatures of Bolshevism would have it. Even had Lenin been 'democratic-centralist' in intent, he could not have been so in practice, since there was no mechanism for imposing the rule of exiled party leaders on a network of small, widely scattered, secretly organised socialist groups with whom communications were intermittent and highly tenuous. Indeed, any such thing would have been madness, for the leadership was in no position to know how, say, the Baku

---

41. Piatnitsky 1935, 52, 69.

oil-workers, the Moscow textile-workers, or the Petersburg engineering-workers should best operate in the circumstances confronting them. Any attempt to presume such knowledge from an exile enclave in distant Zurich (or wherever) would, given the intensity of police repression, have been the height of irresponsibility, quite possibly exposing activists to arrest and whole groups to liquidation.

Here is Piatnitsky:

> The initiative of the local party organisations, of the cells, was encouraged. Were the Bolsheviks of Odessa, or Moscow, or Baku, or Tiflis, always to have waited for directives from the Central Committee, the provincial committees, etc., which during the years of the reaction and of the war did not exist at all owing to arrests, what would have been the result? The Bolsheviks would not have captured the working masses and exercised any influence over them.[42]

The July Days of 1914

Lenin's genius was embodied in the Bolshevik faction of the Russian Social Democratic Labour Party which he led from 1902 to 1917. The Bolsheviks were a network of proletarian activists with a clear mission: to unite the masses, support their struggles, and fan the flames into a revolutionary conflagration powerful enough to destroy the Tsarist regime. Sometimes it was a matter of bare survival for tiny, scattered, hounded groups of revolutionaries in the most forbidding of circumstances.

---

42. Faulkner 2014. I quoted this in a blog article without a reference, and I cannot now find the source, so must crave the reader's indulgence. It is in Piatnitsky somewhere!

Other times it was a matter of opening the gates of the party to thousands of angry young workers brought to life by a great upsurge of struggle from below. As circumstances changed, to remain what they aspired to be – the revolutionary leadership of the Russian proletariat – the Bolsheviks had to be flexible, responsive, able to adapt, yet at the same time immune to both 'liquidationism' (a collapse into reformist acceptance of the existing social order) and 'ultra-leftism' (issuing slogans and calls to action that were too radical to evoke a mass response in current circumstances). Getting the balance right was a matter of constant adjustment as circumstances changed.

The 1905 Revolution had involved Lenin in a head-on collision with the party's Old Guard, who feared 'dilution' in a sea of new members. The defeat of the revolution created a far more serious crisis. 'The years of Stolypin's counter-revolution', reported Zinoviev,

> were the most critical and most dangerous in the party's existence … the party as such did not exist; it had disintegrated into tiny individual circles, which differed from the circles of the 1880s and early 1890s in that, following the cruel defeat that had been inflicted upon the revolution, their general atmosphere was extremely depressed.[43]

Under the hammer blows of repression, many Mensheviks became explicitly liquidationist, arguing for the abandonment of illegal work, the dissolution of underground networks, an exclusive focus on the economic struggles of the workers, and political support for the liberals in the Duma, the Tsarist semi-parliament set up in 1906. Many Bolsheviks, however,

---

43.   Zinoviev 1923/1973, 165.

drew the opposite conclusion, arguing that a new revolutionary upsurge was imminent, that the underground was the only proper field of action, and that the Duma and other Tsarist institutions should be boycotted. Lenin opposed both the liquidators on the right and the sectarians on the left. 'Since the accursed counter-revolution has driven us into this accursed pigsty [the Duma],' he declared, 'we shall work there, too, for the benefit of the revolution, without whining, but also without boasting.'[44]

The argument was not easily carried. 'The whole of our party was fragmented into groups, sub-groups, and factions', recalled Zinoviev. 'In those hard days our central task consisted in assembling the party piece by piece, preparing its rebirth, and, above all, defending the principles of Marxism against all possible distortions.'[45] The aim was always the same: proletarian insurrection in the cities, peasant revolution in the countryside, the overthrow of Tsarism. But strategy had to conform to the prevailing balance of class forces, with tactics geared to the confidence, consciousness, and combativity of the workers. Until the revolution burst forth again, even the Tsarist Duma could be used as a platform for propaganda. But only for that, as Lenin made clear: 'The Bolsheviks regard direct struggle of the masses ... as the highest form of the movement, and parliamentary activity without the direct action of the masses as the lowest form of the movement.'[46]

The downturn lasted from 1907 to 1911. Then the strike rate doubled in a year, and the movement seemed to be reviving. The regime overreacted. On 4 April 1912, with 6,000

44. Cliff 1975/1986, 252.
45. Zinoviev 1923/1973, 164.
46. Cliff 1987, 8.

workers on strike in the Lena goldfields in Siberia, the police opened fire and shot down more than 500 people. Nothing like it had happened since Bloody Sunday in January 1905. More workers – 500,000 – struck in protest in April 1912 than in the whole of the preceding four years. Nor was it momentary rage. May Day that year saw a massive 400,000-strong protest, and the industrial and political unrest continued for the next two years, reaching its peak in the first half of 1914, when almost 1.5 million workers took strike action, a level comparable with 1905. Most of the strikes were openly political.[47]

The Bolshevik Party surged. Lenin, determined to drive the liquidators out of the RSDLP, organised a party congress in Prague in January 1912. Other Social Democratic factions refused to attend (organising an alternative congress in Vienna in August). The result was that the Bolsheviks took full control of the RSDLP, since their party opponents, 'the August Bloc', lacked any real influence in the underground movement inside the country. The two tendencies – the split at the top, the balance on the ground – henceforward reinforced each other. Ideologically unified around an uncompromising rev-olutionary programme – encapsulated in the party's 'three whales': the eight-hour day, the confiscation of landed estates, and a democratic republic – the Bolsheviks now consolidated their grip on the advanced workers. Reformists and intellec-tuals drifted away. The party became at once more Bolshevik and more proletarian.[48] It also became younger: the veterans in their thirties (rarely older) were reinforced after 1912 by a flood of new members in their teens and twenties.[49]

---

47. Kochan 1967/1970, 161–2; Cliff 1975/1986, 319–22.
48. Le Blanc 1993/2015, 156–78.
49. Le Blanc 1993/2015, 183.

Alexander Shlyapnikov, another veteran working-class activist, returned from exile in April 1914 and got a job in an engineering factory in the Vyborg district of St Petersburg. The place was in ferment. Life was an endless round of leafleting, paper drops, solidarity collections, clandestine discussions, mass meetings, strikes, rallies, demonstrations, clashes with the police.[50]

> Every conflict, small or large, irrespective of its origin, provoked a protest strike or walk-out. Political meetings and skirmishes with the police were everyday occurrences. The workers began to make contacts among the soldiers at the nearby barracks ... An extremely active part ... was taken by women workers, the weavers and mill-girls: some of the soldiers were from the same villages as the women workers, but for the most part the young people came together on the basis of 'interests of the heart' ... It was totally impossible to turn such troops against the workers.[51]

By early July 1914, Petersburg was on the brink of revolution. A token strike called by the Bolsheviks in solidarity with the oil-workers of Baku in the distant Caucasus erupted into a massive confrontation when state forces opened fire in the streets of the capital. The entire proletariat was soon in action as 300,000 workers joined a week-long general strike. Veterans of 1905 advised on the erection of barricades and wire entanglements using knocked-down telegraph poles. Factory workers blocked streets by overturning carts and lacing them with wire. Children ripped up cobblestones, and young

50.   Shlyapnikov 1923/1982, 1–8.
51.   Shlyapnikov 1923/1982, 6–7.

workers hurled them at the Cossacks and the police. Across the city there were mounted charges, beatings, shootings, mass arrests. But when the workers returned to work, they did so unbeaten, their mood buoyant, expectant.[52]

> Everyone was overjoyed and encouraged by the recent strike, which had united a huge army of labour in one vivid upsurge of anger. This solidarity could not be smashed either by the police, or by the 'glorious' Cossackry, or by the threats of starvation from the coalition of factory-owners ... Everyone felt that a decisive and nationwide battle was just around the corner.[53]

But it was not. Suddenly, as if by magic, the movement dissolved into nothing. The Tsar had declared war on Germany, and the revolutionary mood was transformed into patriotic fervour. On 2 August, a huge crowd, wholly different in demeanour from those manning the barricades a few days before, assembled in the square outside the Winter Palace. White uniforms appeared briefly on the balcony and then retired – perhaps testing the popular mood? Then others appeared, and, reports the British journalist and writer Arthur Ransome, who was there,

> this time the Tsar was indeed among them, showing himself to the people for the first time in many years, to be greeted with extraordinary emotion and a tremendous singing of the national anthem. The strikes of a few days before were forgotten. War, as so often before and after, had for

---

52.   Shlyapnikov 1923/1982, 9–13; Kochan 1967/1970, 161–5.
53.   Shlyapnikov 1923/1982, 13.

the moment welded the nation into one, or had seemed to weld it.[54]

The Tsar's declaration of war had been a gamble. How would an insurrectionary people react? Would they rally round the Tsar? Or would they follow the revolutionaries and proclaim the international solidarity of the working class?

Russia's corrupt, vicious, tottering regime now had its answer. War had cauterised revolution. Nationalism had suffocated socialism. Portraits of the Tsar had replaced the banners of Bolshevism. Soon, millions would be marching to the front.

---

54.   Ransome 1976, 168.

CHAPTER FOUR

The Great War

Russian peasant-conscripts (in German captivity). Millions were
consumed in industrialised carnage for profit and empire.

The Guards Army was Russia's military elite: 65,000 strong, they had been held back from the front line until now, having been designated the Tsar's personal reserve. But the one-month-old Brusilov Offensive was losing momentum. The success had been stupendous. It had been Russia's greatest victory of the war. The enemy had suffered 1.5 million casualties and been pushed back 50 miles. But the Russians had lost half a million men, their logistics were breaking down the further they advanced, and the Germans had rushed reinforcements from the Western Front to bolster their Austro-Hungarian allies. So the Guards were now sent into the line.

But their attack was mismanaged – by an incompetent high command packed with aristocratic favourites – and they found themselves chest-deep in a swamp, where they were destroyed by the relentless machine-gunning of swarms of German planes. 'The wounded sank slowly in the marsh, and it was impossible to send them help', wrote one senior observer. 'The Russian command for some unknown reason seems always to choose a bog to drown in.' In two weeks, during the horrendous Battle of Kowel, the Guards Army lost 80 per cent of its men. Soon afterwards, as the enemy lines continued to thicken and the autumn rains rendered the swamps impassable, the Brusilov Offensive closed down in renewed stalemate.[1]

So numerous were the rotting corpses in the swamps of Kowel that the Russians sought a truce to clear them away. It was often thus on the Eastern Front. Hecatombs of Russian dead. 'No-one knows the figures', wrote Field-Marshal Hindenburg after the war. 'All we know is that sometimes in our battles with the Russians we had to remove the mounds of

---

1.   Lincoln 1986, 250–7.

enemy corpses from before our trenches in order to get a clear field of fire against fresh assaulting waves.'[2]

Modern industrialised warfare

Russia's greatest victory was also Russia's last throw. Embroiled in a war of mass and machines, a war of attrition decided by industrial power, Russia, despite its prodigious economic development since 1890, lacked the factories and railways to fight a modern war. The First World War was the culmination of a military revolution. The infantryman of 1914 could fire ten times as fast and at five times the range of his predecessor a century before. Heavy machine-guns, with ranges of two miles, could spray 250 bullets across a 500-yard expanse in a single minute. Field guns, with ranges of four miles, could maintain a steady four rounds a minute – firing shells filled with high-explosive, shrapnel, or gas. Such firepower created an impenetrable 'storm of steel' and an 'empty battlefield'. Men crawled from shell-hole to shell-hole, sheltered in the rubble of bombed-out buildings, or tunnelled into the ground. To reach them, guns became heavier and more numerous, and attacks would be preceded by terrific bombardments in which trenches, dug-outs, and bunkers were blasted apart.

Industrial output was decisive: the demand was always for more guns, more shells, more explosive. Mass production provided the uniforms, equipment, guns, munitions, and supplies to sustain armies of millions. Brusilov began his offensive in 1916 with 600,000 men: an army five times the size of the Russian army at Borodino in 1812. His total casualties were 15 times greater. These figures are dwarfed by those for

2.   Lincoln 1986, 259.

the war as a whole. In 1914, the Russian army numbered five million; by the end of the first year, a million had been killed, wounded, or captured. Before the war ended, the Russians would have mobilised no less than 12 million, of whom 75 per cent would have become casualties. This was the scale of the world's first modern industrialised war.

Tsarist Russia was unequal to the challenge. The breakdown began immediately with a crushing defeat at Tannenburg in East Prussia in the first month of the war, then a second at the Masurian Lakes in September; each time, the Russians lost 125,000 men, ten times the losses of the Germans. Further defeats followed in 1915, first at Augustowo in February, then at Gorlice-Tarnow in May-June, when the entire front collapsed and the Tsar's armies retreated 300 miles; total Russian casualties for the year – killed, wounded, and captured – were estimated at two million.[3]

The reasons were obvious. Though each Russian conscript had, on average, to travel three times as far as his German counterpart to reach the front, European Russia's railway density was only a tenth that of Germany's. In addition, Russia had less rolling stock than her enemies, her trains moved at only half the speed, and her rail system could accommodate barely a third the number of trains on each section of track. Provision of motor transport was yet more dire: only 420 transport vehicles for an army of five million at the start of the war. In any case, most Russian roads were unpaved tracks that turned to mud in winter. It could take units stationed in Central Asia two months or more to reach Europe's Eastern Front. When they got there, it was sometimes impossible to arm them. The Russian army began the war a million rifles

3.   Dupuy and Dupuy 1970, 942, 950–2.

short, and with ammunition reserves a billion cartridges lower than the recommended minimum. The state of the artillery was worse: the Germans and Austrians frequently enjoyed a four-to-one battlefield advantage in gun-power, and the Russian cannon often fell silent for lack of shells.[4]

The supply situation deteriorated as the strain of war increased. Medical services for the avalanche of wounded and crippled men were soon overwhelmed. The wounded were dumped on the ground in rain and mud, piled up on freight-car floors and abandoned, or shipped to filthy, overcrowded, disease-ridden hospitals managed by a corrupt military bureaucracy and staffed by untrained personnel. In the front line, uniforms and boots fell to bits and could not be replaced; many soldiers had nothing more than canvas wrappings on their feet in the winter of 1914/15. Two years later, when the mood in the trenches was mutinous, soldiers refused to advance, shouting at their officers, 'Give us boots and warm clothing first!' Arms production was also in crisis as flows of coal and iron failed to match demand: in early 1915, Russian factories were producing only 40,000 rifles a month when battlefield losses were running at six times the rate. General Alexeyev considered it an achievement worth reporting when, in January 1916, as many as seven in ten of his front-line infantry were equipped with rifles.[5]

The Brusilov Offensive was the fruit of one of those great surges from deep inside Russia that can be triggered by defeat and invasion. The Tsarist regime and Russian industrialists collaborated to create a more efficient, state-managed war economy. By the spring of 1916, the annual production rate for

4. Lincoln 1986, 24, 54–8.
5. Lincoln 1986, 94–7, 101–7, 259–60.

rifles was 1.3 million, for machine-guns 11,000, for cartridges 1.5 billion, for field guns 5,000, and for artillery shells 20 million. An additional two million men had been drafted, and most of these were held back from the front line and given extensive training.[6]

But this prodigious effort was matched on the far side of no-man's-land. The stalemate of 1915 had prompted all the warring powers to ramp up their manpower and munitions, and to plan for great offensives, on an unprecedented scale, in 1916. And the truth is that the Brusilov Offensive – victory though it was – wrecked the Russian army. For the impetus of the initial breakthrough was absorbed, a new line of trenches solidified, and the war entered its third winter.

The elites – the courtiers, generals, landowners, and industrialists – had proclaimed the war as a noble struggle for Tsar, Holy Russia, the Orthodox Church, and the Pan-Slavic cause: a cocktail of feudal mumbo-jumbo and blood-and-soil mysticism. At first, voices of reason, in Russia as elsewhere, were drowned in the reactionary tide. 'Despite our attitude toward the government's policy,' announced the liberal Cadet leader Pavel Milyukov,

> our first duty is to preserve the integrity and unity of our country, and to defend her position as a world power. Let us remember well that, at this moment, our first and only task is to support our soldiers, inspiring them with faith in the rightness of our cause, with calm courage, and with hope in the triumph of our arms.[7]

---

6. Lincoln 1986, 241–2.
7. Lincoln 1986, 44.

That 'cause' was, of course, the cause of bankers, profiteers, and imperialists. Russia's industrialists were tied by a thousand golden threads to French finance-capital. Some 80 per cent of Russian capital was foreign-owned, and the largest share was held by French capitalists, who controlled 60 per cent of the country's pig-iron production, 50 per cent of its coal production, and 55 per cent of the reserves in the St Petersburg banks. This gave the Franco-Russian military alliance a firm economic foundation.[8] Not that Russian capitalists were without good reasons of their own for supporting the war. As demand for military supplies soared, so did profits. Hundreds of millions of roubles flowed through a swelling system of speculation and enrichment at the top, while the apparatus of wartime repression crushed working-class resistance to keep hours long and wages low. 'Enormous fortunes arose out of the bloody foam', wrote Trotsky.

> The lack of bread and fuel in the capital did not prevent the court jeweller Faberget from boasting that he had never before done such a flourishing business. Lady-in-waiting Vyrubova says that in no other season were such gowns to be seen as in the winter of 1915/16, and never were so many diamonds purchased ... Nobody had any fear of spending too much. A continual shower of gold fell from above. 'Society' held out its hands and pockets, aristocratic ladies spread their skirts high, everybody splashed about in the bloody mud – bankers, heads of the commissariat, industrialists, ballerinas of the Tsar and the grand dukes, Orthodox prelates, ladies-in-waiting, liberal deputies, generals of the front and rear, radical lawyers ... All came running to

8.   Serge 1930/1972, 45–6.

grab and gobble, in fear lest the blessed rain should stop. And all rejected with indignation the shameful idea of a premature peace.[9]

Much more was anticipated at the war's end. With a seat at the victors' feast, the Russian imperial elite hoped for an ample share in the planned re-division of the world. Bismarck once remarked of Italy that she had 'a large appetite but bad teeth'. He might have said the same of Russia in 1916. Tsarist statesmen dreamed of an enlarged Eastern European empire more ambitious in scope than anything planned by their German or Austrian enemies. Poland (then partitioned between the three Eastern powers) was to be reunited 'under the sceptre of the Russian Tsar'. Galicia was to be taken from Austria-Hungary, and much of Posen, Silesia, and perhaps East Prussia from Germany. The intention was not only to grab territory rich in resources, but to cripple German power for a generation, and to trigger the breakup of the Austro-Hungarian Empire. Equally covetous eyes were laid upon the decaying Ottoman-Turkish Empire to the south, where the Russians wanted Istanbul and the Bosphorus, control of Armenia, and influence in Persia.[10]

But a great unknown cast its shadow over these heady visions of imperial domination. A shadow that grew darker as the war ground on, the death toll mounted, the privation increased, the corruption spread, and the gangrenous nature of the regime and its ruling class became more apparent in the chaos. The great unknown was the mind of the *muzhik* – the Russian peasant.

---

9.   Trotsky 1932–3/1977, 46–7.
10. Stevenson 2004, 137–41.

Eleven out of twelve Russian conscripts were peasants. When called to the colours, 96 per cent of draftees had reported for duty. But what they thought about the war remained a mystery. For, as Milyukov put it, 'In the depths of rural Russia, eternal silence reigned.' What did the silence mean? The cities had shouted loudly for war; politicians, generals, industrialists, and newspapers had all been in favour. But beyond that – in a Tsarist police state where free expression was a crime – who could tell?

The mood of the *Narod* was history's secret. Especially that of the village *Narod*. The peasantry, as Social-Revolutionary Party leader Viktor Chernov put it, had always been 'the sphinx in the political history of Russia'.[11] And never had the silence of the sphinx been more ominous. For the peasantry had been armed. Russia's eight million serving conscripts might be, for the time being, soldiers of the Tsar in an imperialist war. But what if something stirred in their dark hearts? What if, somehow, they came to a contrary view: that the real enemy was not in fact the Kaiser, but the profiteer and the landlord? Might they not then become the armed vanguard of peasant revolution?

The great betrayal

The war had come suddenly. Despite the arms race, the jingo press, and rising tension in the years before, few expected war in the summer of 1914. When people heard the news that an Austrian royal had been assassinated in a remote Balkan town – the Archduke Franz Ferdinand in Sarajevo on 28 June – hardly anyone imagined that this event would lead to world

---

11.   Lincoln 1986, 44–8.

war in five weeks. This included Europe's socialists, even though many – like the Polish-German revolutionary Rosa Luxemburg – had for long argued that the contradictions of the global imperialist order made a terrible war increasingly probable.

For Luxemburg and her comrades, the war came as a double shock. The German Chancellor had been holding private meetings with the leaders of the SPD and the unions. Despite its radical rhetoric, the leadership of the German labour movement was essentially bureaucratic and reformist. On 1 August 1914, in return for a government pledge not to ban them, the union leaders agreed not to call strike action in the event of war.[12] On 3 August, fearing a Russian invasion, their own political isolation, and the possible destruction of the party by military dictatorship, the SPD parliamentary caucus voted almost six to one in favour of approving government war credits – funds for arms – in the Reichstag the following day.

A week before, the SPD Executive had boomed anti-militarist defiance: 'The class-conscious German proletariat ... raises a flaming protest against the criminal machinations of the warmongers ... Not a drop of any German soldier's blood must be sacrificed to the power hunger of the Austrian ruling clique, to the imperialist profiteers.' Hot air: the only real test of anti-militarism is war itself. By 3 August, as leading SPD right-winger Eduard Bernstein recalled,

it was now exclusively a matter of deciding whether at a time when the enemy had already entered the country and [that enemy] anyhow was Russia, a party representing a full third of the German people could deny the means of defence and

12.   Strachan 2001/2003, 122–3.

protection to those called upon to defend them and their families ... Impossible.[13]

On 4 August, the Reichstag voted unanimously for war credits, the SPD's anti-war minority obeying party discipline and voting with the majority. The contradiction in the politics of the party between nationalism and socialism – between the interests of a national-capitalist bloc and those of the inter-national working class – had been resolved. Twenty million would die in consequence.

The SPD leaders' betrayal gutted working-class resistance to the war drive and delivered their supporters into the hands of the *Junker* officer-caste. During the last major international crisis, in 1911, SPD peace rallies had drawn up to 250,000 people. Three years later, at a rally on 28 July 1914, there had again been 100,000 anti-war demonstrators on the streets of Berlin. Across Germany, during four days of mass protest in the last days of peace, there were no less than 288 anti-war demonstrations involving up to three-quarters of a million people. The SPD leadership stopped this movement dead in its tracks. The German working class did not go willingly to war: it was led there, grim-faced, by its own leaders.[14]

When Lenin (in Zurich) read the report of the Reichstag vote in the SPD paper *Vorwärts*, he assumed it was a forgery. Trotsky (in Vienna) was equalled stunned: 'The telegram telling of the capitulation of the German Social Democracy shocked me even more than the declaration of war.'[15] Shlyapnikov had to deal with the bewildered reaction of the

---

13.   Nettl 1966/1969, 367–9.

14.   Sender 1940, 52–3; Strachan 2001/2003, 119–24.

15.   Cliff 1976, 2–3.

advanced workers inside Russia. Because 'it was from the Germans that all Social Democrats of that time "learned" how to be socialists', the expectation had been that the SPD would lead the European anti-war movement:[16]

> when we learned what was happening, it struck us as an absurdity. Newspaper articles spoke about the leaders of German Social Democracy justifying the war and voting for war credits. Our first thought was that the government wire-services were false, and that they wanted to whip us Russian Social Democrats into line ... Workers showered us with questions as to the meaning of the behaviour of the German socialists, whom we had always presented as models for ourselves. Where was all that world solidarity? ... It took a lot of effort to explain to thinking workers that betrayal by some must not lead to universal betrayal, as only capitalists would stand to gain from that. It was vital to restore international contact between workers over the heads of the leaders.[17]

This would not be easy. War has its own momentum. Two moods take hold. Once armies are mobilising, there is fear – the visceral fear of invasion, killing, rape, destruction, displacement. Primeval nightmares of the barbarian horde, of ferocious soldiery, of untrammelled violence become motors of action. The other mood is aggression, hatred, an urge to kill, a mood fostered by a flood of hysterical propaganda demonising the enemy. To these impulses may be added the general excitement engendered by war. Trotsky watched with

---

16. Shlyapnikov 1923/1982, 25.
17. Shlyapnikov 1923/1982, 16–17.

bemusement the reaction in Vienna to the outbreak of war. What was it, he asked, that drew a bootmaker's apprentice, Popischil, half German, half Czech, or the local greengrocer, Frau Maresch, or the cabman Frankl to a patriotic demonstration in front of the War Ministry?

> People whose lives, day in and day out, pass in a monotony of hopelessness are many; they are the mainstay of modern society. The alarm of mobilisation breaks into their lives like a promise; the familiar and long-hated is overthrown, and the new and unusual reigns in its place. Changes still more incredible are in store for them in the future. For better or worse? For better, of course. What can seem worse to Popischil than 'normal' conditions?[18]

There was, perhaps, a brief moment when the war might have been stopped. But with the SPD leaders' capitulation to Prussian militarism, the moment passed. Middle-class Germany came onto the streets to cheer for Kaiser and Army, the backward workers followed them, and the anti-war revolutionaries found themselves isolated and beleaguered.

Just seven people attended a meeting in Rosa Luxemburg's Berlin apartment on the evening of 4 August. Only one person – Clara Zetkin – cabled immediate and unreserved support from among the 300 to whom Luxemburg sent telegrams after the meeting.[19] The anti-war movement appeared to be dead. And with the mighty SPD now cheerleaders for the Kaiser's war, the other European socialist parties collapsed like dominoes.

---

18. Trotsky 1971/1975, 240–1
19. Nettl 1966/1969, 372.

THE GREAT WAR ◆ 101

The anti-war movement

The July movement – Russia's 'semi-revolution' – evaporated.
Most activists were young and liable for military service: many
were called up and went to the front. Others, like the Petrograd
metalworkers, were in 'reserved' occupations, but now, in
wartime, they found themselves 'under military conscrip-
tions and so governed by military regulations'.[20] The small
official space given to radical voices since 1905 was blocked
off. The anti-war newspaper *Pravda* had been suppressed in
July, and a new underground paper, *Sotsial-Demokrat*, had to
be set up and smuggled in from the outside. Informers led
the secret police to an underground Bolshevik conference in
November: everyone was arrested. Later the same month, the
five Bolshevik members of the State Duma were arrested and
condemned to hard labour in Siberia. This, explained Alexei
Badayev, one of the arrested deputies, completed 'the rout of
all revolutionary organisations'. The factories protested.

> But ... the working class had not the strength to undertake
> any far-reaching movement; the war terror was clutching
> the country by the throat, and all revolutionary activity
> entailed either death by court-martial or long periods of
> penal servitude. The arrest of the faction meant that the
> chief party centre in Russia was destroyed. All the threads of
> party work had been centred in the Duma 'five' and became
> now disconnected.[21]

---

20. Shlyapnikov 1923/1982, 35.
21. Badayev 1929/1987, 211–25.

State security worked hand-in-glove with industrialists to smash labour organisation. Militants were blacklisted and either dismissed or conscripted into the army. Meal breaks were shortened and works canteens monitored to prevent meetings; some bosses even installed gramophones to play loud music and drown out discussion![22] As wartime orders flowed in, the employers extended the working day, made overtime compulsory, scrapped health safeguards, and lobbied for 'the militarisation of labour'. Women, children, peasants, and foreign workers entered the factory on low wages, depressing established rates, dissolving old networks of solidarity. Even prisoners-of-war and convicts were pressed into service. War, profit, and 'patriotism' formed an alliance to ratchet up the rate of exploitation.[23]

But the war churned the deep waters of Russian society like no previous national crisis. The newspaper threat of 'German domination' was soon displaced by a real experience of hunger. The transport system broke down, food supplies failed, and prices skyrocketed beyond the reach of city workers. By late 1915, Petrograd was receiving only a quarter of the rail shipments it required. A third of the city's bakeries closed for lack of flour and oil. Two-thirds of the butchers had no meat for sale. That winter, women queued for hours in sub-zero temperatures to buy handfuls of food and fuel. The following year, peasant riots erupted across the grain-growing provinces of European Russia. Shops were looted in protest against shortages and inflation. Meantime, unwilling to sell at fixed government prices when there was nothing to buy, the peasants hoarded or consumed the food they produced.

---

22. Shlyapnikov 1923/1982, 80–3.
23. Shlyapnikov 1923/1982, 89–91; Lincoln 1986, 107–8.

A 'scissors crisis' that would recur: whenever the supply of manufactured goods from the cities failed, so did the return flow of agricultural produce from the villages.[24]

Though war fever had overwhelmed the class struggle in the summer of 1914, the effect was superficial. To be cowed is not to concede. The advanced workers' reaction to the war was sullen suspicion. Alexander Shlyapnikov was riding on an overcrowded tram in August 1914 when a man 'who looked like a police clerk' launched into an anti-Semitic tirade: all the 'Yids', he told fellow passengers, should be arrested as German spies. The Bolshevik answered him. A row erupted and blows were exchanged. The tram stopped and the police were called. Shlyapnikov was asked to alight, but the working-class passengers rallied to his side, refusing to let him be taken away, and the conductor tugged the bell and the tram moved off.[25] A tiny incident: but like the speck of light in the distance that signals the approach of an express train in the night, this scuffle on the top deck of a tram in which Petrograd workers sided with a revolutionary against a racist heralded the mighty conflagration to come.

The Bolsheviks recovered quickly from the shock of 'the great betrayal'. The Petrograd RSDLP Committee had an anti-war leaflet out within days. 'Workers of the world, unite!' it began. 'To all workers, peasants, and soldiers! Comrades!'

A bloody spectre hangs over Europe. The capitalists' greedy competition, the politics of violence and plunder, dynastic calculation, and fear for privileges in the face of the rising international workers' movement are driving the

24.   Lincoln 1986, 207, 219–20, 297.
25.   Shlyapnikov 1923/1982, 27.

governments of all countries along the path of militarism
… 'Down with the war!' 'War on war!' must roll powerfully
across city and hamlet alike … Workers must remember
that they do not have enemies over the frontier: everywhere
the working class is oppressed by the rich and the power
of the property-owners. Everywhere it is oppressed by the
yoke of exploitation and the chains of poverty.[26]

The Bolshevik underground needed no 'centralist' direction.
The party's anti-war politics were an automatic reaction: the
activists on the ground knew what to argue. But it was Lenin
who gave the internationalist position its classic exposition.
Facing squarely the crisis of the world war, taking to its logical
conclusion the reality that the worker's enemy was the boss,
the landlord, and the policeman – not the German or Austrian
conscript – he opposed both the chauvinism of the ruling
class and the pacifism of milk-and-water 'internationalists',
proclaiming instead 'revolutionary defeatism'. A victory for
Tsarism would strengthen the regime. Support for the Tsarist
war-effort would undermine the class struggle. Therefore the
defeat of Russia was to be welcomed. The imperialist war
between the great powers was to be transformed into a civil
war of workers and peasants against their own ruling classes.

Any 'peace programme' will deceive the people … Not
'peace without annexations', but peace to the cottages, war
on the palaces; peace to the proletariat and the working
people, war on the bourgeoisie! … An oppressed class
which does not strive to learn to use arms, to acquire arms,
only deserves to be treated like slaves … Our slogan must

26. Shlyapnikov 1923/1982, 20.

be: arming of the proletariat to defeat, expropriate, and disarm the bourgeoisie.[27]

Between January and June 1916, the exiled Bolshevik leader worked on a long pamphlet, *Imperialism: The Highest Stage of Capitalism*. Written for working-class activists, its purpose was to explain the world war in the context of contemporary capitalism. At the heart of Lenin's conception was the growing concentration of capital in giant corporations, creating monopolies and cartels which dominated the world economy. Because of its dependence on loans to fund investment, industrial capital had merged with finance capital. And because of their scale, the resulting industrial-financial conglomerates needed overseas markets for the export of both commodities and capital. This brought them into competition with each other on a global scale; and it was this struggle for markets and colonies that explained the arms race and the world war.[28]

For Lenin, the world war – this vortex of mass industrialised killing on an unprecedented scale – was the bitter fruit of a new stage in the development of capitalism, one in which the system was divided into rival national-capitalist blocs, each dominated by giant corporations, each heavily armed, each competing for a re-division of the world in the interests of profit. Here was the theoretical underpinning of the anti-war instincts of the advanced workers in Russia.

The battles of 1915 had consumed two and a half million. To those killed, maimed, or captured was added a rising toll of deserters. 'Many men are running away', wrote one soldier. 'In one platoon of 65 men, there are now only 30, because 35

27.   Cliff 1976, 3–5.
28.   Faulkner 2013, 174–7.

have deserted.' 'The number of soldiers travelling without documents on the railroads is increasing', reported General Ivanov. There were 'hordes of soldiers wandering through towns and villages, along railroads, and, in general, across the face of the entire Russian land', complained the Minister of Agriculture. But when the Tsarist military attempted to draft male breadwinners from the peasant villages, the resistance was violent. The police were mobbed and bricked at the assembly points. 'Go ahead and shoot', people shouted. 'Better that we should die here than be sent to war without bullets!' Those taken often jumped the trains at stations and headed back home. 'When we finally stopped at Uvarovka,' reported one escorting soldier, 'it turned out that 372 out of 800 had escaped.'[29]

The factories and the proletarian suburbs smouldered with discontent. Moscow's workforce had grown by a tenth each year of the war, Petrograd's by a fifth. At first, the new proletarians were rendered docile by the shock, the unfamiliarity, the lack of roots, the absence of a tradition of resistance. Not for long. Police repression, long hours, dangerous conditions, low wages, shortages of food and fuel, the overcrowding in the workers' districts, all combined to educate the newly proletarianised in the malevolence of the system that held them bound. Between April and September 1915, almost 800 strikes involving 400,000 workers cost Russia's bosses a million days of lost production. From then on, strikes were frequent; and sometimes the contagion spread to the soldiers. A hundred workers had been shot down by soldiers firing into a crowd chanting 'Down with the war!' in Ivanovo-Voznesensk in September 1915. But men of 181st Infantry Regiment joined

29.   Lincoln 1986, 179–82.

a crowd of 30,000 striking workers in singing the *Marseillaise* at Petrograd's Finland Station in October 1916. A red light was flashing for Russia's *ancien regime*.[30]

The social crisis was going critical. The political tension became electric. It affected all levels of society. The court camarilla of the Tsarina and Rasputin found itself friendless even in the gerrymandered State Duma. Vladimir Purishkevich – an arch-monarchist, proto-fascist, and rabid anti-Semite – lambasted a regime of favourites and lickspittles in which ministers had to 'throw themselves at the sovereign's feet, beg the Tsar for permission to open his eyes to the horror of the current state of affairs, and plead with him to deliver Russia from Rasputin and all his corrupt band'.[31]

The assessment was universal, but few expressed it so openly, and fewer still were willing to act. Purishkevich was an exception, as were Prince Felix Yusupov and the Grand Duke Dmitri Pavlovich. These three luminaries of the Russian Right, along with two others, an army captain and a doctor, conspired to lure Rasputin to Yusupov's palace in order to murder him, baiting their trap with the prospect of a night with the Prince's beautiful young wife.

A semi-basement room was made into a sumptuous salon for the reception, with tapestries, Chinese vases, a bearskin rug, and much fine furniture. A steaming samovar of tea, bottles of Madeira and Marsala, and plates of cream cakes were provided. The wine and the cakes were laced with cyanide.

Rasputin was led to the room and invited to drink and eat pending the arrival of the Princess. He was eventually persuaded to consume several glasses of wine and some cream

30. Lincoln 1986, 189, 220, 225–7.

31. Lincoln 1986, 304.

cakes. To the horror of his hosts, they had no discernible effect. Yusupov then fetched a revolver, returned to the salon, and shot 'the filthy, depraved, corrupt peasant' in the heart. Rasputin let out a roar and collapsed on the bearskin rug. It seemed he was dead. The plotters relaxed. Then, suddenly, Rasputin hauled himself to his feet and staggered out of the palace into the night. Purishkevich pursued him, armed with a revolver. It took four shots to bring the fugitive down. Even then he lay unconscious, but still alive. Rasputin only finally expired when the plotters heaved his body into the ice of the River Neva. It was about 3.30 on the morning of 16 December 1916.

The comic-opera revolution of the Russian aristocracy changed nothing. The conspirators had hoped to solve the terminal crisis of Old Russia with a phial of poison. But the assassination of a religious mystic could hardly be expected to redeem the entire rotten Romanov regime. The Tsarina's favourite minister, the sycophantic Alexander Protopopov, closed the matter with the announcement that he was in communication with Rasputin's ghost. Tsarism staggered its last few steps to the abyss guided by a spectre.[32]

Ten weeks later, the real revolution began. It was led by the working women of Petrograd.

---

32.   Trotsky 1932–3/1977, 94; Lincoln 1986, 304–10.

PART TWO

The Tempest, 1917

CHAPTER FIVE

The February Revolution

Mass participatory democracy. The Petrograd Soviet in session.

The first day: 23 February

No-one expected it. Lenin, in exile in Zurich, told a meeting of young socialists a month beforehand that 'We of the older generation may not live to see the decisive battles of this coming revolution.'[1] No-one planned it or called for it. 'Not one party was prepared for the great overturn', wrote the Menshevik Sukhanov. 'The Revolution was a great and joyous surprise for us', reported the Social-Revolutionary Zenzinov. 'No-one thought of such an imminent possibility of revolution', recalled the Bolshevik Kayurov.[2] The day – International Women's Day – was to be marked only by meetings, speeches, and leaflets. Even the Vyborg Committee of the Bolshevik Party in the heart of proletarian Petrograd opposed the call for strikes. The danger of a clash with the police, and a bloody defeat, was too great.[3]

The revolutionaries were behind the curve. They had missed the meaning of the 9th of January. On the anniversary of 1905's Bloody Sunday massacre, 150,000 workers from a hundred factories had come onto the streets of the capital. It had turned into a massive protest against war, inflation, and low wages. The Petrograd demonstration was mirrored elsewhere: 30,000 out in Moscow, 14,000 in the Baku oil fields, 10,000 in Kharkov in the Ukraine. The one-day protest had then turned into a strike wave, rolling on for weeks, gaining momentum. By the end of January, a quarter of a million workers had taken action, the simple demand for bread mixing

---

1.   Chamberlin 1935/1965, 131.
2.   Chamberlin 1935/1965, 73.
3.   Trotsky 1932–3/1977, 121.

with political demands for an end to the war, the overthrow of the government, a second revolution.[4]

But strikes sap the fighting power of the workers. The weapon had to be kept sharp. So no strikes had been called when the 23rd of February dawned. The bread lines had already formed, many working women up since three, standing grim-faced in the bitter cold. It could take four hours to secure two rolls. Or it might take four hours to secure nothing as the 'No More Bread' sign was posted. Then 12 hours in the mill or the metal-bashing shop.

The working women of Petrograd were doubly oppressed: ground down in the workplace by wretched conditions, long hours, and low pay; ground down at home by the toil and poverty of everyday existence. Many were on their own, their brothers, husbands, and sons conscripted. Many were grey with hunger and exhaustion. Sometimes they would go two or three days without eating. Sometimes they would cross themselves and weep with joy when they managed to buy bread.[5] When a loaf can induce tears, revolution is close.

It began in these lowest depths of proletarian Russia. Seven thousand low-paid women workers of the Vyborg District's textile mills came onto the streets demanding 'Bread'. They marched to neighbouring factories and called them out. By ten o'clock, 20,000 were on strike. By noon, 50,000. That afternoon, the numbers swelled further as men from the engineering factories joined them. Before the day was out, 90,000 were involved, and crowds of women and teenagers were smashing open the food shops in two districts of the city.[6]

4. Lincoln 1986, 317–18.
5. Lincoln 1986, 320–1.
6. Lincoln 1986, 321.

What did it mean? No-one could be sure. Less than a quarter of the city's workers had taken part, and the action had been confined to the northern Vyborg and Petrograd Districts. In particular, the male engineering workers at the Putilov factory, 40,000 strong, the largest and most militant workforce in Russia, had not gone onto the streets. There had been no clashes, no casualties.

The authorities were well prepared should matters escalate. Under the overall authority of the Minister of the Interior, Alexander Protopopov, the city was divided into six police districts. Three lines of defence had been set up to deal with unrest: police, Cossacks, and the soldiers of the military garrison. The police were armed paramilitaries, most on foot, some mounted. The Cossacks – traditional Tsarist cavalry recruited from the minor gentry and rich peasants of the southern prairies – were armed with whips, sabres, pistols, and carbines. All told, there were 12,000 police and Cossacks. But if these failed, there were no less than 150,000 soldiers stationed in the city.[7]

Neither the revolutionaries nor the authorities rated the events of 23 February much different from many others over the preceding six weeks. The former still issued no calls to action. The latter took only limited security measures. Extra flour was sent to some of the large bakeries. Troops were deployed to guard key points across the city. Whips were issued to the Cossacks. That was all. Most would probably have agreed with Zinaida Gippius, the avant-garde poet and hostess, who considered the day's events just an 'ordinary sort

7.   Chamberlin 1935/1965, 74.

of hunger riot'.[8] No-one had yet grasped the inner meaning of Women's Day 1917.

The second day: 24 February

The following morning, central Petrograd was calm. The authorities relaxed. But too soon. Though the call had not come from their leaders, grassroots activists had been at work through the night, agitating for strike action and mass demonstrations on the morrow. 'We must go ahead and solve our problem by force', one of them proclaimed at an early morning mass meeting of metal-workers at the Stetinin Factory. 'Only in this way will we be able to get bread for ourselves … Arm yourselves with everything possible: bolts, screws, rocks. Start smashing the first shops you find!'

Before nine o'clock that morning, 40,000 Vyborg workers attempting to march into the city centre were confronting 500 police and Cossacks at the Aleksandrovsky Bridge. Across four city districts, tens of thousands were on the move, bringing the total on strike to double the number of the first day. The Nevsky Prospect, the main downtown thoroughfare of elite Russia, was choked with demonstrators who had flooded in from the proletarian suburbs. As well as the slogan 'Bread!', others could now be heard: 'Down with the autocracy!', 'Down with the war!' At the bridge, on the Nevsky, and at a dozen other places, there were clashes with the police. Again and again, the 'Pharaohs' – as they were known – launched ferocious charges to break up groups of workers. Sometimes the groups scattered and reformed elsewhere; sometimes they

---

8. Lincoln 1986, 262–3, 322–3.

held their ground with volleys of cobblestones and lumps of ice.

The police never go over to the crowd. They are recruited from the most backward section of the working class. Their role is to defend the property and power of the rich against threats from below. Their daily work is a matter of hostile collisions with activists, workers, and the poor. Their hatred of the oppressed is reinforced by what is nowadays called 'canteen culture'. So they become a hardened reactionary caste, immunised against any appeal for solidarity by a psychic armour of indifference and prejudice. In revolution, the police cannot be won over; they have to be physically confronted and routed.[9]

What, though, of the Cossacks? Though conservative property-owners, and often detailed to internal security, they were first and foremost soldiers. Their demeanour was different from usual – there was not the sneering, the pent-up aggression, the smouldering threat of violence. Sometimes there were even smiles and winks. More. A policeman struck a woman with a knout. A Cossack chased him off. Or so went the rumour passed along in the crowds. On the Aleksandrovsky Bridge, the Cossack line did not give way, but it proved permeable. Some crossed on the Neva ice; and were not stopped. Others darted beneath the Cossacks' horses; and they were not stopped either. The workers at the Erikson factory held a meeting, voted to strike, and came out 2,500-strong onto the Sampsonievsky Prospect. In a narrow place they met the Cossacks. But when ordered to charge, the Cossacks formed files behind their officers and passed peacefully through the crowd. The drama was enacted several

9. Farrell 1992, passim, esp. 48–88, 165–8.

times, always with the same outcome. 'Of discipline,' Trotsky later commented,

> there remained but a thin transparent shell that threatened to break through any second. The officers hastened to separate their patrol from the workers, and, abandoning the idea of dispersing them, lined the Cossacks across the street as a barrier to prevent the demonstrators from getting to the centre. But even this did not help: standing stock-still in perfect discipline, the Cossacks did not hinder the workers from diving under their horses. The revolution does not choose its paths: it made its first steps toward victory under the belly of a Cossack's horse.[10]

Uncertainty remained about what these two days of turmoil portended. 'Nothing serious' in the view of British Ambassador George Buchanan, reporting to the Foreign Minister in London.[11] Though 28 policemen were reported beaten up (the workers injured went unrecorded), no firearms had been used and no-one had been killed.[12] Perhaps matters would yet pass over without a major clash?

Nonetheless, General Sergei Khabalov, head of security in the capital, ordered further precautionary measures. Known revolutionaries were to be rounded up. The Guards Reserve Cavalry was summoned to the capital. More soldiers were to be deployed to back up the police and the Cossacks. But should firearms be used? A critical question that could not be answered. Would what Napoleon once called 'a whiff of

---

10. Trotsky 1932–3/1977, 124–5.
11. Chamberlin 1935/1965, 76.
12. Trotsky 1932–3/1977, 125–6.

grapeshot' clear the streets? Or would shooting detonate an explosion in the volatile mass of proletarian Petrograd? No-one could tell. Certainly not Interior Minister Protopopov, who, it is recorded, spent the evening trying to contact Rasputin's ghost.[13]

The third day: 25 February

Early on the third day it was clear that the strike was spreading and becoming general. Many smaller factories were now closed. Shops were shuttered, trams at a standstill, newspapers no longer available. University and high-school students had joined the movement. The police estimated 240,000 on strike, a third more than on the previous day. The Putilov men – a 40,000-strong proletarian phalanx – now joined the movement. Locked out of the factory in a labour dispute, they stormed the gates, held a mass meeting, and formed a 'provisional revolutionary committee' to 'lead the struggle against the police, to organise fighting detachments, and to establish revolution in the streets'.[14]

By midday, tens of thousands had gathered near the Kazan Cathedral on the Nevsky Prospect. The workers had padded their backs and shoulders with rags, towels, and bits of blanket as protection against whips. They carried knives, metal spikes, and broken bottles as weapons. Impromptu street meetings were taking place in different places. What followed was chaotic. According to Trotsky:

13. Lincoln 1986, 325.
14. Trotsky 1932–3/1977, 127; Chamberlin 1935/1965, 76; Lincoln 1986, 326.

The mounted police open fire. A speaker falls wounded. Shots from the crowd kill a police inspector and wound the chief of police and several other policemen. Bottles, petards, and hand-grenades are thrown at the gendarmes. The war has taught this art. The soldiers show indifference, at times hostility, to the police. It spread excitedly through the crowd that when the police opened fire by the Alexander III monument, the Cossacks let go a volley at the horse Pharaohs ... and the latter had to gallop off.

Elsewhere, a group of strikers led by the worker-Bolshevik Kayurov took off their caps and approached a line of Cossacks, appealing for solidarity in the struggle against the Pharaohs for the right to eat.

'The Cossacks glanced at each other in a special way,' Kayurov continued, 'and we were hardly out of the way before they rushed into the fight.' And a few minutes later, near the station gate, the crowd were tossing in their arms a Cossack who before their eyes had slaughtered a police inspector with his sabre.[15]

Then the soldiers appeared, a line of grey greatcoats tramping forwards, faces glowering beneath fur hats, rifles levelled, bayonets fixed, a wall of state power. But the wall was crumbling. The workers approached them, getting close, posing questions. Why have you come? Who is your enemy? Which side are you on? Where do your interests lie?

---

15.   Trotsky 1932–3/1977, 127–8; Lincoln 1986, 325–6.

The soldiers are sullen. A worm is gnawing them, and they cannot stand it when a question hits the very centre of the pain.

On one side were the sons of peasants in uniform; on the other, the sons of peasants in workers' blouses. And not just men. There were many women in the crowds. Women who were mothers, sisters, wives, and girlfriends of the soldiers. Or perhaps just other women who reminded the soldiers of their families. To shoot Germans who were shooting back had been bad enough, for these had been men with whom they had no quarrel, conscripted to fight as they were, taking the same shit from officers. Now those same officers wanted them to shoot down starving women on the streets of Petrograd. These women were in front of them now, taking hold of their rifles, speaking eye-to-eye. 'Put down your bayonets! Join us!' they implored.

> The soldiers are excited, ashamed, exchange anxious glances, waver; someone makes up his mind first, and the bayonets rise guiltily above the shoulders of the advancing crowd. The barrier is opened, a joyous and grateful 'Hurrah!' shakes the air. The soldiers are surrounded. Everywhere, arguments, reproaches, appeals. The revolution makes another forward step.[16]

On this day, the third of the uprising, the police had been defeated. The crowd had fought back against their violence, the Cossacks had attacked them, the soldiers failed to support them. In the Vyborg, the police stations had been wrecked,

---

16.   Trotsky 1932–3/1977, 128–9.

some officers lay dead, the rest had fled. But the matter remained in the balance. The Cossacks and the soldiers were wavering – allowing crowds to assemble and pass, even protecting them from the police – but not a single unit had yet gone over to the uprising. It was not yet a revolution. And, as Trotsky put it, 'the fate of every revolution at a certain point is decided by a break in the disposition of the army. Against a numerous, disciplined, well-armed, and ably led military force, unarmed or almost unarmed masses of the people cannot possibly gain a victory.'[17]

The core of the capitalist state is formed of bodies of armed men and women. You could strip away everything else except for soldiers, police, and prisons, and you would still have the state. Everything else is optional, but a minority ruling class cannot rule without armed force. They need this both to defend their property and profits from radical movements at home, and to defend their empires and 'national interests' abroad. The Tsarist state of February 1917 was no different in this respect than any of Europe's other warring states. But its historical peculiarities – the fact that the Tsarist state was more autocratic and thuggish than, say, the British or the French; a fact rooted in the medieval backwardness of Old Russia – meant that it was now cracking apart. What gnawed most deeply in the mind of the soldiers was the crude brutality of the Tsar's army, the bloody mash of a hopeless war, and the age-old agony of villages crippled by rent, debt, and land-hunger.

'The psychological moment when the soldiers go over to the revolution is prepared by a long molecular process, which, like other processes of nature, has its point of climax' (Trotsky). But at that point, the workers must push forwards

---

17. Trotsky 1932–3/1977, 139–40.

with confidence to convince the soldiers that they can win. For a soldier to mutiny, especially in time of war, is more perilous than for a worker to strike. To disobey officers, to refuse to fire, to break ranks, to join the crowd: to do these awesome things – to suddenly and completely burst the iron bands of military discipline – the soldier must be certain that he will become part of a victorious mass able to protect him.[18] The next two days would decide.

The fourth day: 26 February

It was a Sunday, not a working day, so the people rose late. Petrograd was quiet that morning. 'The city is calm', the Tsarina cabled the Tsar. 'Today, 26 February, the city is entirely peaceful', reported General Khabalov.[19]

The city centre was under military occupation. Overnight, the Tsar had telegraphed new instructions to Khabalov:

I ORDER YOU TO BRING ALL OF THESE DISORDERS IN THE CAPITAL TO A HALT AS OF TOMORROW. THESE CANNOT BE PERMITTED IN THIS DIFFICULT TIME OF WAR WITH GERMANY AND AUSTRIA. NICHOLAS.

Khabalov had passed these orders to his subordinates, Petrograd's district police and army chiefs, and they had made their dispositions. The downtown area had been turned into a military camp. Infantry detachments garrisoned key government buildings. Armoured cars were parked at strategic points. Machine-guns had been placed to sweep major inter-

18.   Trotsky 1932–3/1977, 139–42.
19.   Trotsky 1932–3/1977, 132; Lincoln 1986, 329.

sections. Cossack squadrons were held in readiness to clear the streets. 'If the crowd is small,' Khabalov had told his officers, 'if it is not at all aggressive, and if it is not carrying [red] banners, then use your cavalry detachments to disperse it. But if the crowd is in any way threatening, and if it carries banners, then you are to act according to regulations. Give three warnings, and then open fire.'[20]

The workers had been massing in the proletarian suburbs since dawn, but it was late morning before the first processions approached the lines of soldiers covering the roads and bridges into the city centre. Wherever marchers ignored orders to halt, officers gave the order to fire.

Shooting erupted in different parts of the city, and the workers scattered into doorways, courtyards, side-streets. Brown humps were left on the road, streaked with red. Machine-guns opened up. The Cossacks moved down the streets.

The workers could not defend themselves: they had come to the demonstration unarmed. Shlyapnikov, one of only three members of the top Bolshevik leadership in the city, had firmly opposed the demand that the workers should arm. The workers could not defeat the soldiers with guns. They had to win with arguments. Only thus might the insurrection be victorious: 'I decisively refused to search for arms at all and demanded that the soldiers should be drawn into the uprising, so as to get arms for all the workers. This was more difficult than to get a few dozen revolvers. But in this was the whole programme of action.'[21]

---

20.   Lincoln 1986, 327–9.
21.   Chamberlin 1935/1965, 76.

But now the soldiers were shooting, and, as one of them recalled, 'the blood of workers stained the snow'.[22] Shlyapnikov's strategy appeared to some a failure. Revolution takes place in a fog of uncertainty. Each protagonist sees only a small part of the whole; each attempts to fill out the picture with impressions, rumours, fragments of reports, the random assessments and opinions of others. What few could see at first was that the killing – which was intended to render the embryonic revolution abortive – was in fact the psychic trauma that finally shattered the brittle allegiance of the soldiers.

The regime had chosen to militarise the crisis. It was attempting to restore order through terror: by turning Russian soldiers against Russian workers. But this was a gamble. The state is an apparatus of power based on social relationships. A combination of coercion and consent – force and fraud – it depends for its integrity, on the one hand, on the quiescence of the majority, and on the other, on the loyalty of the personnel of its repressive agencies. By 26 February 1917, the Tsarist state had lost the former: the proletarian crowds were now openly revolutionary, demanding an end to the war and the autocracy, and, even in the face of machine-guns, were standing their ground and spitting defiance. And the signs were there that the size, confidence, and appeals of those crowds were acting like an acid on the threads of discipline binding soldiers to officers in the grey lines opposite.

Many soldiers were firing high. Some were not firing at all. 'Each man must fire in turn so that I can watch him shoot', yelled an enraged officer. 'Aim at the heart!'[23] In many parts of the city, the revolutionaries in the crowds, the rank-and-file

---

22. Lincoln 1986, 329.
23. Lincoln 1986, 331.

leaders, sensed the wavering in the ranks. Sometimes it was obvious to all. The Menshevik Nikolai Sukhanov witnessed an encounter on the Trinity Bridge. A cordon of Grenadiers was standing shoulder-to-shoulder barring the way. Activists were directing speeches at them. The soldiers were listening, some solemn and attentive, others chuckling. The workers were very close, and though the soldiers generally prevented anyone passing, a few filtered through and were not turned back.

There was no direct insubordination, but they were obviously unsuitable material for any active operations, and there was clearly nothing for the officers to do but turn a blind eye on this scene of 'corruption'. For this detachment to take aim and open fire on the people it had been conversing with was unthinkable, and no-one in the crowd believed for a moment that it was possible.[24]

This was confirmed by an unequivocal event that evening. Accounts of it vary, but what seems to have happened is this. Someone got news to the fourth company of the Pavlovsky Regiment – which had been confined to barracks without access to newspapers, telephones, or visitors – that its three sister companies were firing on the people. By six o'clock a decision had been made, and 150 men of the fourth company went onto the streets without orders, commanded by an NCO (his name lost to history). Their aim, it seems, was to recall their comrades. On the way, they encountered a police detachment. Either it was barring their way or it was shooting on unarmed demonstrators – or both – and the Pavlovsky men opened fire on the police, killing one, wounding another. Further details of

24.   Sukhanov 1955/1984, 26–7.

their journey are obscure, but when they returned to barracks, they were surrounded by the Preobrazhensky Regiment, shots were exchanged, and the rebels were forced to surrender. Thirty-five were arrested and locked up. Another 22, however, had absconded – with their rifles.

Sukhanov heard an eyewitness account of these portentous events at the house of writer Maxim Gorky, a regular meeting-place of the city's radical intelligentsia. 'This', reported Sukhanov,

> was the first instance of a massive open clash between armed detachments ... the importance of this affair ... was enormous and quite unmistakable ... to the Pavlovsky Regiment belongs the honour of having performed the first revolutionary act of the military against the armed forces of Tsarism ... This was a terrible breach in the stronghold of Tsarism.[25]

The fifth day: 27 February

Much had happened in the night. Soldiers had discussed the day's events in a hundred heated exchanges in the barracks. Many were sickened by what they had done, and embittered against the officers who had ordered it. Many had reached a firm decision: they would not fire on the crowds again.

The military mutiny began at seven o'clock. The previous day, the men of the Volynsky Regiment's training squad had opened up with rifles and machine-guns in Znamenskaya Square, killing 40, wounding as many. The psychic injury was deep. Now there was atonement. 'Fathers, mothers,

25. Sukhanov 1955/1984, 28–9.

sisters, brothers, even brides, are begging for bread', Sergeant Kirpichnikov told his comrades. 'Should we strike them down? Have you seen the blood running in the streets? I propose that we do not march against them tomorrow ... Enough blood has been shed. Now it is time to die for freedom.'[26]

When Captain Lashkevitch arrived to lead out his detachment, he was met with cries of 'We will not shoot'. The whole regiment refused to move. Their officers fled. Shots were fired at them from the windows as they went. The barracks had been taken for the revolution.

But could it be held? Soon the Volynsky were rushing to the neighbouring barracks – of the Litovsky, the Preobrazhensky, the Lithuanian Guards, the 6th Military Engineers – calling out their fellow soldiers just as the working women had called out their fellow workers on the first day.

Separate movements were under way in other parts of the city. Inner struggle convulsed the Moscow Regiment. Some officers and the training battalion tried to bar the way from Vyborg to the city centre, but other soldiers of the regiment joined the workers in a brief exchange of fire. Soon the whole regiment simply dissolved into the crowd, the soldiers helping to hunt down the police, break into the arsenals, and find arms for the workers.

By early afternoon, the insurgents had taken 40,000 rifles, 30,000 revolvers, and 400 machine-guns. Armoured cars had appeared flying red flags. The fortresses had been opened and political prisoners released. Resistance at the barracks of the army bicyclists on the Sampsonievsky had been overwhelmed by the fire of armoured cars and machine-guns; a fence was broken down, buildings set on fire, the commanding officer

---

26. Lincoln 1986, 331.

killed, and other officers either captured or forced to flee through some vegetable gardens.

Late in the day came news that the Semenovsky Regiment – which had shot down the workers on Bloody Sunday in 1905 – had joined the revolution. They in turn called out the Izmailovsky.[27]

Successive attempts throughout the day to form loyalist detachments with which to confront the mutineers and the workers failed. Khabalov had dispatched a regiment of a thousand men under a resolute officer with orders to suppress the uprising by whatever means were necessary. The regiment simply disappeared and was never heard from again. Entire military formations were dissolving. The once rock-solid human material of the Tsarist state had turned into a social fluid that seeped away in all directions. Thus, as Trotsky observed, 'The Tsarist garrison of the capital, numbering 150,000 soldiers, was dwindling, melting, disappearing. By night, it no longer existed.' Khabalov cabled the Tsar at army headquarters:

> I beg to inform His Imperial Highness that I am not able to carry out his instructions about the restoration of order in the capital. The majority of army units, one after the other, have betrayed their oaths, refusing to fire upon the rebels. Other units have joined the insurgents and have turned their weapons against the troops still remaining loyal to His Highness.[28]

---

27.   Trotsky 1932–3/1977, 143–4; Chamberlin 1935/1965, 78–80; Lincoln 1986, 331–2.

28.   Trotsky 1932–3/1977, 146–7; Lincoln 1986, 333.

The triumph of the revolution in the Tsarist capital was complete by nightfall on 27 February. The strike was now general across the city and involved virtually the entire proletariat of 400,000 workers. The mutiny was equally general: it is estimated that somewhere between 15 and 45 per cent of the soldiers were on the streets with the workers, and virtually all the rest were in their barracks refusing orders to take repressive action.[29]

But Petrograd was a city of two million in a country of 150 million. What of the rest of Russia?

There are circumstances in which a revolutionary city advances too far ahead of the country of which it is part and is then isolated and crushed. It happened with Paris in 1848 and 1871. It would – as we shall see – be a danger narrowly averted in Petrograd itself in July 1917, and a danger terribly realised in Berlin in 1919. Progress in politics is impossible without a vanguard. But a vanguard must be one step ahead, not three.

Not that anyone would have been to blame had Petrograd moved too far ahead in February 1917. It was both the politico-military and the proletarian centre of Russia: at once the administrative core of the Tsarist state and the front line of the anti-Tsarist class struggle. Here, in the ancient capital, the contradictions of Old Russia attained their most concentrated form, accumulating a most powerful explosive charge. The danger of a premature detonation was there. But the elemental social forces unleashed in the February Days could not be held back. No-one summoned them. Many of the revolutionary leaders – Mensheviks, Social-Revolutionaries, and especially Bolsheviks – were abroad. Second-rank figures filled the gaps. But no call to the streets had come from any of them.

29.   Cliff 1976, 82.

One rank-and-file Bolshevik reported: 'Absolutely no guiding initiative from the party centres was felt ... the Petrograd Committee had been arrested and the representative of the Central Committee, Comrade Shlyapnikov, was unable to give any directives for the coming day.'[30] This is confirmed by the testimony of the *Okhrana*, the Tsarist secret police, whose files were seized after the revolution. An undercover agent inside the Bolshevik Party send this report to his superiors on 26 February:

> The movement which has started has flared up without any party preparing it and without any preliminary discussion of a plan of action. The revolutionary circles began to react only toward the end of the second day when the desire to develop the success of the movement to the widest limits possible became noticeable ... The general attitude of the non-party masses is as follows: the movement started spontaneously, without any preparation, exclusively on the basis of the food crisis.[31]

This does not mean there was no leadership: it means that the leadership was from below. All mass action has to be organised. No meeting, march, or street battle lacks its leaders. Sometimes they had emerged from the ranks, thrown up by the February crisis. But more often it was veterans of the struggle, members of the revolutionary underground, who formed the organisational backbone of the uprising. Most were Bolsheviks. In answer to the question 'Who led the February revolution?', Trotsky gave an unequivocal answer: 'Conscious

---

30. Trotsky 1932–3/1977, 163.
31. Cliff 1976, 84.

and tempered workers educated for the most part by the party of Lenin.'[32]

The spark had caused a conflagration. But would Russia catch fire? The issue was only briefly in the balance. Strikes and demonstrations began in Moscow on 27 February. That very afternoon, detachments of soldiers arrived at the City Duma to enquire how they might join the revolution. Some sporadic shooting occurred over the succeeding few days, but it was nothing to compare with Petrograd's heavy toll (1,443 killed and wounded).

The revolution in the provincial cities was delayed a little more, beginning only on 1 March; but the story was everywhere the same. The workers left the factories, marched to the city centre, and gathered round the council chamber. The soldiers joined them there. The crowds waved red banners, hailed the revolution, and sang the *Marseillaise*. Petrograd answered for Russia. The vanguard was but one step ahead.[33]

What of 'Bloody' Nicholas? Having lost control of the garrison of the capital, the Tsar ordered fresh regiments to advance on Petrograd. The requirement was for 'an absolutely loyal, though not necessarily large force'. The Cavaliers of St George – a battalion of decorated veterans – were detailed for the operation, along with four infantry regiments, four cavalry regiments, two machine-gun units, and four batteries of artillery. As the news from the capital worsened, further units were put on standby. But it proved a shadow army destined never to arrive. Far more dangerous than machine-guns was the moral contagion flowing in all directions from Red Petrograd. General Alexeyev resolved to keep his soldiers out of range.

32. Trotsky 1932–3/1977, 171.
33. Trotsky 1932–3/1977, 156–60.

The necessity now was for a political move, not a military one, lest the army as a whole be lost.

Of this, though, the imbecilic head of the dynasty was incapable. Instead, he abandoned his headquarters, his generals, and his front-line army, intent on returning to his family at Tsarskoe Selo Palace on the edge of Petrograd. He never reached it. The Tsar's train was diverted by railway workers and, having shunted aimlessly across the countryside for two days, finally came to rest at Pskov.[34] The Tsar of All Russia could no longer even accomplish a train journey. Thus was the 300-year-old Romanov dynasty terminated in a railway siding.[35]

34. Lincoln 1986, 334–7.
35. The Tsar's family was held captive by revolutionary forces and eventually executed at Yekaterinburg on 17 July 1918 to prevent their liberation by White (counter-revolutionary) forces during the Civil War.

CHAPTER SIX

Dual Power

The July Days. Demonstrators scatter as right-wing gunmen
open fire from upper-floor windows.

The First Provisional Government

It had been one of the greatest popular revolts in history. The battle had been waged entirely through the mass action of the *Narod*, the common people of Russia. The bourgeoisie – the financial, commercial, and industrial capitalists – had played no part whatsoever. The middle class – the civil servants, the upper professionals, the intelligentsia – had watched events unfold from their balconies. The socialist leaders had either said nothing at all, or they had said nothing that made any difference. There was no leadership of any kind 'from above'. The workers and peasant-soldiers of Petrograd had made the revolution all by themselves, as it were 'from below', and the rest of plebeian Russia had followed their lead.

Yet power now passed not to the workers, but to the liberal-bourgeois politicians of the Cadet Party, organised as a 'Provisional Committee' (soon to become 'Provisional Government') of the Tsarist Duma – a fake parliament of 'lords and lackeys' elected on a restricted franchise heavily weighted in favour of the rich. The new government was the work of Pavel Milyukov, a history professor and head of the Consti-tutional Democrats (or Cadets), a liberal party of the middle class and intelligentsia favouring constitutional monarchy. The Cadets had formed a 'Progressive Bloc' with the Octobrists, a pro-Tsarist party of the nobility and the bourgeoisie whose leading figure was a rich Moscow finance-capitalist called Alexander Guchkov.

Behind the scenes, as the action unfolded on the streets, Milyukov had spent five sleepless days trying to construct a Progressive Bloc government – a new conservative regime to restore order, defend property, and continue the war. His first effort was an abortive attempt to replace Tsar Nicholas (who was soon under house arrest) with his brother Mikhail – that is, to swap one autocrat for another. Mikhail, fearing for his own safety, refused to play his assigned role. It was then that Milyukov sat down and wrote out a list of ministers. It was a cabinet of Duma conservatives dominated by the Cadet Party. It included one token socialist: Alexander Kerensky.[1] This, then, was a government of landlords, industrialists, and right-wing professors. It seemed that the mountains in labour had given birth to a mouse. Trotsky called it 'the paradox of the February Revolution'. What had happened?

Another power had in fact come into existence: the Soviet of Workers' Deputies (soon to become the Soviet of Workers' *and Soldiers'* Deputies). The 1905 Revolution had taught this lesson: that the common people in action can best be organised by a pyramid of participatory democratic assemblies, the lowest bodies comprising mass meetings of everyone in a factory, barracks, battleship, or whatever, these electing delegates to the higher bodies.

But whereas the 1905 Soviet (the word simply means 'council' or 'assembly') had originated as a strike committee – in other words, had emerged 'from below' out of the class struggle itself – the 1917 Soviet was an initiative of the radical intelligentsia. As the more moderate socialists emerged from semi-underground existence or were freed from prison by the crowds, they gathered in the grandeur of the Taurida Palace, the meeting place of the Duma, and formed a 'Provisional Executive Committee of the Soviet of Workers' Deputies'. They called an immediate assembly and invited the workers to send delegates; but those who had taken the initiative had

1. Lincoln 1986, 339–51 passim.

earned much credit – and they were, after all, proven activists, many with records of prison and exile – so the instigators of the movement were confirmed as its leadership.[2] These men held the real power in the capital after the February Days, for they enjoyed the confidence of the revolutionary crowds. But instead of wielding it, they stood aside and invited the Duma liberals to form a government. Was this not, after all, a 'bourgeois revolution'?

The Provisional Government immediately became the rallying point for right-wing forces. The President, Mikhail Rodzianko, was an ageing courtier, an ardent monarchist, and a mediocrity. The Prime Minister, Prince Lvov, was a rich but somewhat obscure right-wing liberal. The War Minister was Guchkov, who, as head of the Central Military-Industrial Committee, was effectively Russia's war-profiteer-in-chief. But the real leadership was provided by Milyukov, the new Foreign Minister, described by the Menshevik chronicler of the revolution, Nikolai Sukhanov, as 'the soul and brain of all bourgeois political circles'.[3]

Milyukov was an inveterate imperialist and warmonger – which, in the radically changed circumstances, required that he now become also a serial liar, issuing statements to the Russian people that were 'only for domestic circulation', while assuring the British, French, and Italian Ambassadors that 'Russia would fight to the last drop of her blood'. The Russian bourgeoisie's commitment to the war was absolute. It was dependent on the Entente for bank loans and arms shipments. The state had been bankrupted by the war, the economy reduced to a state of near-collapse, such that Milyukov and his colleagues could

2. Sukhanov 1955/1984, 38–40.

3. Trotsky 1932–3/1977, 198–209.

not imagine continuing without foreign support. In any case, they wanted a seat at the victors' banquet when the war ended; above all, they wanted Istanbul and the Bosphorus, as both an outer defence-work and a seaway to global markets.

The war was the most pressing issue, but it was not the only one dividing the Provisional Government from Red Petrograd and the wider revolutionary mass movement. The workers wanted higher wages, an eight-hour day, an end to shortages, and, increasingly, control over production. The peasants wanted the land – the land of the gentry, and land free of debt and other burdens. And the minority peoples of the Tsarist Empire – 55 per cent of the population – wanted autonomy and an end to chauvinism, racism, and national oppression. The Provisional Government represented the opposite: war, empire, the restoration of order, and the defence of private property. Yet it lacked any power to impose them. War Minister Guchkov wrote to General Alexeyev less than a month after the overturn and confessed the true situation:

The Provisional Government possesses no real power and its orders are executed only in so far as this is permitted by the Soviet … It is possible to say directly that the Provisional Government exists only while this is permitted by the Soviet … Especially in the military department, it is possible now only to issue orders which do not basically conflict with the decisions of the … Soviet.[4]

This reality had received dramatic confirmation as early as 1 March, when a packed thousand-strong session of the Soviet, flooded with grey-clad soldier delegates, had passed Order No.

4. Chamberlin 1935/1965, 101.

1. This formalised the soldiers' revolution. It called upon all military units to elect democratic committees, and declared that these would henceforward run the armed services. At a stroke, the rule of the Tsarist officer caste was terminated. The Order further stated that formal equality between officers and men now existed, that officers would no longer be allowed to impose disciplinary punishment, and that common soldiers would enjoy full rights as citizens. Above all, it abolished both corporal punishment and the death penalty, the ultimate barbarisms of a class-based military. Order No. 1 even outlawed abusive language: the routine use of terms like 'mother-fucker' were no longer to be tolerated when officers spoke to soldiers. The Russian soldier, denied dignity through the dark centuries of Tsarism, could finally stand upright.

The Right raged against Order No. 1. Alexeyev complained to Guchkov in mid April that

> Discipline in the Army is declining every day ... The authority of officers has fallen, and there is no power to re-establish it. The spirit of the officers' corps is falling more and more as a result ... of their removal from actual power over their subordinates or the transfer of this authority to the soldiers' committees ... Pacifist sentiment develops in the armies.[5]

The testimony of men like Alexeyev is clear: real power lay with the mass movement represented by the Soviets. Why, then, had the Soviet leaders allowed the Cadets to form the government? Why, moreover, had they done this in the face of many of their own supporters' uncomprehending

---

5. Chamberlin 1935/1965, 107.

indignation? The 'socialist intelligentsia' were soon receiving a stream of protests – like that from a former peasant called Zemskov, a Moscow worker and army deserter who had been hiding in the Kuban region for two years. Writing to Kerensky on 26 March, he denounced the empty claim that 'freedom' had been achieved:

After all, you're oppressing the people, and they have long known that you are riding on their back: the noble and the merchant and the scholar and the poet and the journalist and the lawyer and the priest. You're all nothing but greedy predators making off with the products of our labour. That is what the people are suffering from, and this is where the root of social evil lies. All the people need is for you parasites not to be riding on their back, and once that happens, freed from your yoke, they will govern themselves ... [6]

The two dominant parties on the Executive Committee of the Petrograd Soviet were the Mensheviks and the Social-Revolutionaries. The former had lost their influence among the politicised workers, becoming a party dominated by students, teachers, lawyers, journalists, and the literati. Though still 'Social Democrats' with a theoretical commitment to socialist revolution at some indeterminate point in the future, the Mensheviks were what would now be called 'reformists'. They believed that Russia's revolution was inherently 'bourgeois', that the Cadets were therefore the natural party of government, and that the role of socialists was to advance the cause of labour – to seek reforms – within a new democratic order.

6. Steinberg 2001, 85–91.

The Social-Revolutionaries (SRs) were a party of radical intellectuals formed from a fusion of old Narodnik traditions. They had continued to focus on the peasantry and the land question, and the revolution now carried them high on a great tide of soldier and peasant votes. But they merely embodied in party form the conservatism of rich peasants, the wavering of middle peasants, and the passivity of poor peasants. This fractured and backward class base prevented the Social-Revolutionaries from giving decisive leadership. They would eventually split, the Right SRs backing the Provisional Government, the Left SRs becoming allies of the Bolsheviks.

What both parties shared was 'petty-bourgeois' (lower-middle-class) leadership. The Mensheviks and SRs were radical democrats and social reformers: they were not proletarian revolutionaries intent on the overthrow of the state and the wholesale dispossession of the rich. This political 'Centre' – in relation to the Cadets on the Right and the Bolsheviks on the Left – was variously described by contemporary critics as being composed of 'moderates', 'compromisers', 'defencists', 'liquidators', 'social-patriots/chauvinists', and 'petty-bourgeois democrats'. We shall use the term most familiar to modern readers and call the Mensheviks and SRs collectively 'the Reformists'.

The Reformists conceded power to the Cadets because they feared the radicalism of the popular movement and were unwilling to assume power as the leaders of a revolution. The result was a 'dual-power' regime, in which authority was divided, since the Provisional Government exercised – or attempted to exercise – formal state power, but the great majority of the newly awakened masses of workers, soldiers, and peasants distrusted the Cadets and gave their allegiance to the Soviets, which they regarded as people's parliaments, and to the Reformists, seen as the people's true leaders.

This 'dual-power' regime was highly unstable and could not endure. Politics has no real centre-point, least of all in time of revolution. Every great question demanded a yes or no answer. Would the war be ended? Would the eight-hour day be realised? Would the peasants get the land? Would the nationalities be granted autonomy? To each of these questions, the Provisional Government gave one answer and the masses another. But no final resolution was possible under a dual power with alternative and competing centres of political authority. Either the Provisional Government, in control of the old state apparatus and representing the propertied classes, would crush the Soviets and re-establish the uncontested rule of the rich, or the Soviets, democratic assemblies of the revolutionary masses, would overthrow the Provisional Government and create a new social order.

Sooner or later, the matter would have to be resolved in one way or the other. In the meantime, in relation to this tension between conservative reaction and popular revolution, the Reformists formed an unstable centre – a role that involved them in performing an endless political pirouette on a shrinking social base, as they incrementally lost the support of the masses by their evasion, vacillation, and treachery on the central questions of the revolution.

The dual-power regime was bound to unravel. But it would take time – time for the masses to learn from experience that the Reformists did not represent their deepest aspirations. The advancing consciousness of the masses – moving from right to left during the eight months between February and

October – would henceforward constitute the principal motor of the revolutionary process.

Because it was fluid and fast-moving, the consciousness of the masses would repeatedly leap ahead of the representative bodies elected in an earlier phase of the revolution. This would give rise to a series of crises and clashes punctuating the history of 1917. From this we learn that the relationship between social classes, mass movements, democratic assemblies, and political parties is never straightforward. The interconnections form a working mechanism, in which nothing is fixed, everything is in motion. It cannot be assumed that a political party simply 'represents' a social class in any direct way, or that a democratic assembly merely 'expresses' the general will of a mass movement. Again and again, parties and assemblies lag behind the consciousness of active social forces. To understand the Russian Revolution is to grasp the inner dynamics of a complex political mechanism in a state of perpetual motion.

The April Days

When the Soviet Executive Committee decided to hand power to the bourgeoisie on 1 March, not a single one of its 39 members had voted against, despite the fact that 11 were Bolsheviks or Bolshevik sympathisers. The following day, in a meeting of the full Soviet assembly, of some 400 deputies present, only 19 voted against, though some 40 were members of the Bolshevik faction. The lower ranking Bolsheviks – closer to the masses – tended to be more to the left, but the leadership simply tailed the Reformist-dominated Executive Committee. This tendency was reinforced by the return of two leading Bolsheviks, Lev Kamenev and Joseph Stalin, from exile in mid March. Taking over the party organ, *Pravda*, they moved the Bolsheviks further to the right. The Bolsheviks would support the Provisional Government 'in so far as it struggles against reaction or counter-revolution'. And so long as German soldiers obeyed the Kaiser, the Russian soldier should 'stand firmly at his post answering bullet with bullet and shell with shell'.[7] Nothing of substance separated these Bolsheviks from the Reformists.

As soon as news reached him of the February Revolution, Lenin fretted to find a way back to Russia across war-torn Europe from his place of exile in Switzerland. He and his collaborators eventually secured the permission of the German authorities to pass through their territory in a 'sealed train'. Like a dangerous bacillus, the Bolshevik cadre were to be injected into the Russian enemy, but prevented from contaminating any Germans along the way. Lenin arrived at Petrograd's Finland Station on 3 April. The Bolsheviks had arranged a grand reception. There to meet him were an honour guard of Kronstadt sailors, a division of armoured cars, detachments of revolutionary soldiers, and a large crowd of factory workers. What he had to say thrilled the waiting rank and file and stunned their leaders. Standing on an armoured car, the headlamps casting long shafts of light down the darkened streets, the uplifted faces of thousands of soldiers, sailors, and workers illuminated in the glare, red-and-gold banners flying overhead, he denounced the Provisional Government, called for an immediate end to the imperialist war, and hailed the advent of 'the worldwide socialist revolution'.[8]

---

7.   Trotsky 1932–3/1977, 300–1, 304–5.

8.   Raskolnikov 1925/1982, 68–73.

The very next day, he presented a short written summary of his perspective to a party conference in the Kshesinskaya Mansion, which the Bolsheviks had commandeered as their headquarters. Lenin's *April Theses*, published in *Pravda* three days later, were effectively a manifesto for a second revolution. He denounced 'revolutionary defencism' – the idea that the war should now be supported as a defence of the revolution – on the basis that the Provisional Government was an imperialist government in alliance with other imperialist governments fighting an imperialist war. He rejected any support for the Provisional Government and called for its overthrow and replacement by 'a republic of Soviets of Workers', Agricultural Labourers', and Peasants' Deputies throughout the country, from top to bottom'. This would involve 'abolition of the police, army, and bureaucracy'. All state officials would be elected, subject to immediate recall, and receive average wages. Russia, in other words, was to become a mass partici-patory democracy. The landed estates were to be confiscated and turned into public property. A single national bank was to be set up. A new International was to be founded to spread revolution across the world.[9]

Earlier, in his *Letters from Afar* – the Bolshevik leader's first response to news of the revolution – he had demanded that the working class be armed, creating a people's militia that would maintain order, defend the revolution, advance the cause of 'peace, bread, and freedom', and ensure that 'every worker improved his living conditions, that every family had bread, that no adult in a rich family should have a bottle of milk before the need of every child was satisfied, that rich

---

9.   Lenin 1917b, passim.

apartments, abandoned by the Tsar and the aristocracy, should afford refuge to the poor and homeless'.[10]

Lenin now embarked on a month-long struggle to turn his party round – a month of meetings, big and small, of speeches and articles, of urgent private huddles with leading Bolsheviks. Two days after his *Theses*, for example, came an article on dual power, clarifying the central question of the state:

> In what does this dual power consist? In the fact that side by side with the Provisional Government, the government of the bourgeoisie, there has developed another government, weak and embryonic as yet, but undoubtedly an actually existing and growing government: the Soviets of Workers' and Soldiers' Deputies ... It consists of the proletariat and the peasantry (clad in army uniform) ... It is a revolutionary dictatorship, i.e. a power based on outright revolutionary seizure, on the direct initiative of the masses from below... [11]

To the Reformists, Lenin sounded out of touch, a wild extremist, a raving madman, according to some a 'has-been' peddling 'superannuated truths of primitive anarchism'. The Bolshevik leaders squirmed: 13 out of 16 at first rejected the *April Theses*, and when they were published in *Pravda* there was an editorial disclaimer stating that they reflected Lenin's 'personal opinion', which was 'unacceptable'.[12] Elsewhere, his call for 'worldwide socialist revolution' was denounced as 'Trotskyist'. 'Lenin is wrong when he says the bourgeois revolution is finished', claimed Kamenev. 'The democratic

---

10.   Lenin 1917a, passim; Chamberlin 1935/1965, 132.

11.   Lenin 1917c, 27.

12.   Lincoln 1986, 365.

dictatorship is our foundation-stone', explained Tomsky, another leading Bolshevik.[13] But the argument was quickly won among the party rank and file, the worker-Bolsheviks rooted in the factories. By the time of the Party Congress, held from 24 to 29 April and attended by 149 delegates representing 79,000 members, Lenin's 'left' Bolshevism was hegemonic across the party; Kamenev and Stalin, the chief culprits in the 'reformist turn', were not elected to the party's new five-member steering group.[14]

Lenin's victory at the conference was made easier by a decisive political test: the 'April Days' demonstrations on the 20th and 21st of the month. They were triggered by the Cadet Foreign Minister Milyukov's 'Note' setting out the Provisional Government's attitude to the war. Addressed to Russia's allies, it affirmed the nation's resolve 'to bring the world war to a decisive victory', adding that 'the leading democracies will find a way to establish those guarantees and sanctions which are required to prevent new bloody encounters in the future'. The message was clear: all-out imperialist war and a predatory victors' peace.

The Note 'touched the match to the fuse' (Trotsky).[15] The battleships and the barracks exploded into action. The great naval base at Kronstadt was in the vanguard of Petrograd's revolutionary movement. The crews of entire ships were applying to join the Bolshevik Party, and already there were 3,000 full members and 35,000 registered sympathisers. Up to a thousand men worked on the great battleships of the age, and virtually every job required a high level of training

13. Trotsky 1932–3/1977, 332–3.

14. Trotsky 1932–3/1977, 339–40.

15. Lincoln 1986, 361.

and technical skill. Despite this, food was bad, living quarters cramped, regulations punitive, and officers frequently corrupt and brutal. Such was the class hatred festering in the ranks that some 36 'Dragons' – as sailors called naval officers – had been killed in the February Revolution. Now Kronstadt was a ferment of revolutionary activity. At the naval base, reported the Bolshevik sailor Fyodor Raskolnikov,

Every ship, every regiment, every workshop sought to form a library of its own, however small this might be ... and every political pamphlet was literally read to shreds. The February Revolution has aroused tremendous interest in politics and had thereby evoked an unprecedented demand for Bolshevik literature.[16]

The movement had begun on the afternoon of 20 April. The Finnish Regiment appeared, fully armed, in front of the Marinsky Palace, where the Provisional Government met. It was soon joined by other military units, the crowd swelling to 25,000 or more before the day was out. 'Down with Milyukov!' was the dominant slogan.

News of the demonstration spread widely that evening – to other regiments, to Kronstadt, to the factories – and the following day saw vast columns of soldiers, sailors, and workers converging on the city centre, many bearing arms, many chanting 'Down with the Provisional Government!' and 'Down with the war!' There were clashes with counter-demonstrators, shots were exchanged, and, for the first time since February, blood flowed on the streets of the capital.

---

16.   Raskolnikov 1925/1982, 64–7.

Then, after just two days, the movement subsided. It had been a chaotic, spontaneous, improvised eruption from below. It had revealed the growing gulf between the Provisional Government and the masses: the growing polarisation of Russia into an imperialist Right and a revolutionary Left. Between the two, attempting to bridge the gulf, were the Reformist leaders of the Petrograd Soviet, who were, on the one hand, lobbying the government for a better form of words, while on the other, remonstrating with the crowds to end the protests.

The April Days doomed the First Provisional Government. The Cadets and the Reformists, both desperate to restore public confidence, now favoured a coalition. The Cadets needed left cover for their conservative programme. The Reformists were under pressure to accept governmental authority. The main casualty was Milyukov, too tainted by his blatant imperialism to remain. The lynchpin of the Second Provisional Government would be Alexander Kerensky, now appointed War Minister, a Social-Revolutionary who had been the sole socialist to serve in the First Government.

Kerensky would dominate the next months of the revolution. A master of fiery, flowery, often hysterical rhetoric, he was a charismatic force at the tribunal. A man of tremendous energy but limited intellect, he seemed to float above the revolution, a bombastic voice shouting above its myriad conflicts, having no firm grounding in a social base, a party programme, a set of principles. It was this that fitted him for the role he was to play – neither Cadet nor Bolshevik, neither Right nor Left – as the living expression of the unresolved contradictions of the Russian Revolution in the middle months of 1917.[17]

17.   Lincoln 1986, 367–71.

The July Days

The change of government meant a change of rhetoric: nothing more. Kerensky immediately embarked on a tour of the front, delivering tirades of histrionic patriotism to mass assemblies of soldiers. His mission, he had explained before setting out, was 'to make it possible for everyone to look death in the face calmly and unflinchingly'. 'Forward to the battle for freedom!' he exhorted the soldiers. 'I summon you not to a feast, but to death!'[18] The social-chauvinist Kerensky thus gave to the imperialist war a democratic colouring. The excitable lawyer with a radical past made a more compelling messenger of death than a conservative history professor. But the agenda was the same: Russian peasant-conscripts were to die for Istanbul and the French banks.

Observers were impressed by the oratory and its momentary effect. But it *was* only momentary: the disintegration of the Russian army continued apace. Short of food, clothing, and equipment, lacking sufficient guns and munitions, knowing of the revolution, hoping that it portended a 'Black Partition' of the land, desperate to return to their villages to join in, the peasant-soldiers' will to fight was gone. No-one listened anymore to priests and officers talking of Tsar, Faith, and Mother Russia. But the new slogans, too, were as echoes in the wilderness. What was 'Prussian militarism', 'Austrian oppression', and the 'Turkish yoke' as winter turned to summer and the village at home was making ready for the ploughing? And the supreme question: would they plough the same land this year as last; or would they take the lord's land and plough that too? And would they themselves survive to see it? 'What

---

18.   Lincoln 1986, 404–5.

is the use of peasants getting the land if I'm killed and get no land?' shouted one soldier at Kerensky.

Again and again, they returned to this, huddled in trenches, around their campfires, at meetings of the soldiers' committees, listening to reports of delegates returning from Petrograd with news. Many had met the Germans and the Austrians. The soldiers opposite would call out, 'Rus! Don't shoot!' The Russians would answer: 'We won't if you don't!' And sometimes they would meet to share food, to drink, to make merry: the storm of steel in no-man's-land, the machinery of death, stilled by fraternisation. Maxim Gorky celebrated this in his newspaper:

> It is apparent that the accursed war, begun by the greed of the classes in command, will be ended by the power of the commonsense of the soldiers. If this happens, it will ... give man the right to be proud of himself. His will shall have conquered the most abominable and bloody monster, the monster of war.[19]

Some were fraternising. Many more were refusing to fight. Most significant of all, thousands, then tens of thousands, and finally hundreds of thousands were leaving the trenches to begin the long trek home. Sukhanov, who worked with Gorky in the office of *Novaya Zhizn* ('New Life'), saw 'elemental forces' at work in a movement so vast that it 'recalled to mind a vast migration of peoples ... a huge flood of soldiers took off for home without any sort of permission whatsoever. They clogged all the railroads, terrorised the authorities, threw

19.   Lincoln 1986, 397–403.

passengers off the trains, threatened the entire transport system, and, in general, created a civic disaster.'[20]

On the home front, too, a great struggle against war erupted in the summer of 1917. The opening clash had been launched by the First All-Russian Congress of Soviets of Workers' and Soldiers' Deputies, in session for three weeks in June. Only 105 out of 777 delegates were Bolsheviks. The Mensheviks and Social-Revolutionaries wanted a display of support for 'revolutionary defencism' and 'the unity of the revolutionary movement'. They had just strong-armed the Bolsheviks, increasingly dominant in Petrograd, into cancelling their own planned demonstration. Now they would cap this triumph with an alternative demonstration of their own.

The effort backfired. The protest on 18 June, 400,000 strong, paraded under a great sea of Bolshevik banners. 'Down with the Ten Capitalist Ministers!', 'Down with the Offensive!', and 'All Power to the Soviets!' were the dominant slogans. Isolated handfuls carried Reformist banners. The crowd tore down those bearing the slogan 'Confidence to the Provisional Government!' 'Here and there,' reported Sukhanov, 'the chain of Bolshevik banners and columns would be broken by specifically Social-Revolutionary or official Soviet slogans. But they were drowned in the mass.' The smiles on the platform faded into stony glares as the leaders of the February Revolution were confronted with the unmistakable image of the October Revolution yet to come.[21]

But the war went on. The Right still hoped for victory and the spoils. The Centre dreamed of a democratic crusade that would unite the people behind the new Provisional

20.   Lincoln 1986, 405.
21.   Trotsky 1932–3/1977, 448–66 passim.

Government. Only the Left, Lenin's Bolsheviks, were unequivocal in opposing the war, and this intransigence was fast gaining them the allegiance of Petrograd. At the First Conference of Petrograd Factory Committees in late May/early June, for example – an assembly of rank-and-file delegates representing 337,000 workers – the Bolshevik resolution was supported by 80 per cent of the 570 delegates. Around this time, too, the Bolsheviks secured a majority in the workers' section of the Petrograd Soviet. The Social-Revolutionaries remained dominant among the soldiers, but even here there was a sharp contradiction between the formal support still given to the leaders of the old party of peasant revolt and the practical support given to the slogans and programme of Bolshevism: the political trajectory of the soldiers was obvious.

Further afield, though, the Bolsheviks were still well behind, as their showing in the elections to the All-Russian Congress of Soviets had revealed: only one in seven delegates.[22] This imbalance – between Red Petrograd and the rest of Russia – exploded into a major political crisis when the Provisional Government attempted to move military units from the capital to the front to reinforce its planned summer offensive.

Lenin sensed the danger that Petrograd might become a second Paris Commune, and he argued relentlessly with his supporters to rein back the movement and discourage a premature attempt on power.[23] In this he now found a powerful ally in Trotsky, just returned from exile (and shortly to join the Bolshevik Party, along with his 4,000 adherents, the Mezhrayontsy group, which until now had kept itself aloof

22. Trotsky 1932–3/1977, 432–3.
23. Cliff 1976, 260–1.

from both major Social Democratic factions).[24] But when the news arrived that two-thirds of the 1st Machine-Gun Regiment was to be sent to the front, the struggle against the Provisional Government escaped the control of the Bolshevik leadership. Like the sailors – essentially skilled workers in naval uniform – the machine-gunners were an elite of military specialists who had taken their place in the vanguard of the revolutionary movement. They now called on other regiments and the larger factories to join them on the streets, and in the early hours of 3 July an angry and heavily armed demonstration converged on the Taurida Palace, 25,000 Putilov men with their families marching in from the Narva District to the south-west, 30,000 workers and soldiers from the Vyborg in the north.[25] More were coming. The Kronstadt sailors shouted down the Bolsheviks they usually heeded and applauded Anarchist calls for solidarity. 'Everyone burned with a desire to go and help as quickly as possible', recalled Raskolnikov.

> Their aims were unclear. There was no precise notion of why the machine-gunners were demonstrating in Petrograd. It was enough that a demonstration was taking place. An active feeling of comradeship impelled the Kronstadt masses to take direct action, telling them that at such a moment they should be with their blood-brothers, the workers and soldiers of Petrograd. With such a unanimous collective feeling, it was very difficult to go against the stream.[26]

---

24. Cliff 1989, 203–30 passim.
25. Lincoln 1986, 391–2.
26. Raskolnikov 1925/1982, 141–7.

It was the same everywhere. Typical of the mood was the resolution passed at a mass meeting at the Schlusselburg Powder Works, where 5,000 men and women worked:

Enough hesitations! In the name of freedom, in the name of peace, in the name of the worldwide proletarian revolution, the All-Russian Executive Committee of the Soviet of Workers', Soldiers', and Peasants' Deputies must seize power! Executive power must rest in its hands, for it truly expresses the people's will. There is no other way out of the impasse ... The policy of compromise with the bourgeoisie has clearly revealed how utterly bankrupt and ruinous for the cause of freedom it is.[27]

The danger now was very real of an attempt on power in the capital. The Provisional Government and the Soviet Executive Committee had virtually no reliable military forces at their immediate disposal. But should they face a decisive threat, there was little doubt that sufficient loyalist units could be summoned from the provinces. And were this to happen, the forces of counter-revolution might be unleashed, and Red Petrograd, the vanguard of the popular revolution, would be drowned in blood. Raskolnikov was on the phone to Zinoviev at Bolshevik headquarters seeking advice. What to do? He could not stop Kronstadt marching on the following day. Zinoviev went away to consult. A few minutes later he came back with the answer: the party would lead 'a peaceful and organised armed demonstration'. The Bolsheviks, having failed

27. Steinberg 2001, 182–3.

to restrain the movement, had resolved to place themselves at its head – the aim: to contain it.[28]

It was a vast display of Bolshevik power. Tens of thousands marched with guns – the 1st Machine-Gun Regiment, the Kronstadt sailors, Red Guards (armed workers' militia) from the larger factories, and many others. Hundreds of thousands more marched with them. Perhaps as many as half a million were on the streets of the capital on 4 July 1917. The mood was tense as these vast plebeian crowds moved through the streets of the aristocratic and bourgeois city centre. Then shots were fired by snipers from the upper floors of buildings on the Liteiny Prospect and elsewhere, scattering the crowds, sending soldiers and sailors storming into houses to kill anyone they suspected. The bloody clashes would eventually claim 400 victims. Little wonder that the mood of the crowd around the Taurida Palace was angry and edgy by the end of the day. Victor Chernov, Social-Revolutionary Minister of Agriculture, was seized by sailors when he attempted to give a speech and had to be rescued by Trotsky. 'Take power, you son-of-a-bitch, when they give it to you!' one worker snarled at Chernov.[29]

But they would not. And the two-day siege of the Taurida Palace dissolved, the July movement petering out in backstreet skirmishes between middle-class patriots and revolutionary militants. Then, around midnight, the balance tipped decisively. Regiments that had remained neutral marched to defend the Soviet Executive Committee – the Izmailovsky, the Preobrazhensky, the Semenovsky.

There were many reasons. The scenes on the streets had been chaotic and bloody: many were unsettled and yearned

28.   Raskolnikov 1925/1982, 149.
29.   Trotsky 1932–3/1997, 544–53 passim.

for order. The movement had lacked purpose. The angry worker who had confronted Chernov had expressed it as clearly as anyone: the demonstrators were attempting to force those who refused power to take it. Only the Bolsheviks were for Soviet power, and they were not yet strong enough. And now, into the confusion, to further confound and disorient the retreating movement, was inserted a Great Lie. The regiments that had marched to the defence of Reformism had been told that Lenin was a paid agent of the German Kaiser.[30] This calumny would provide the cover for a storm of reaction and repression designed to destroy the Bolshevik Party – a storm that would clear the ground for an attempted military coup to smash the entire revolutionary movement.

30. Trotsky 1932–3/1977, 558–61.

CHAPTER SEVEN

Counter-Revolution

The counter-revolution.
Right-wing soldiers demonstrate in favour of war.

The Kerensky Offensive

Between the February and July Days, the revolution was in the ascent. The February Days had brought down the Tsarist regime. The April Days had brought down the First Provisional Government of Cadets. The July Days would also work their effect: the Second Provisional Government, a coalition of Cadets and Reformists in which the former predominated, broke up, to be succeeded, after much shilly-shallying of party leaders, by a new coalition, now with Kerensky as Premier and a majority of Mensheviks and Social-Revolutionaries. Kerensky was the keystone of the shaky edifice of this Third Provisional Government. A liberal-imperialist in red feathers, he was the cuckoo in the Soviet, having been the only socialist in the First Provisional Government, the dominant figure in the Second, and now, as head of the Third, the indispensable point of intersection between the old state apparatus and the new revolutionary democracy. But these two forces – the opposing poles of the dual-power regime – were irreconcilable. Kerensky's accommodation to the imperialist bourgeoisie – symbolised by his total commitment to the war – necessitated a full-scale attack on the revolutionary vanguard. The July Days retreat provided the opportunity.

The masses had been growing more organised and radical, better able to distinguish friend from enemy, truth from falsehood, more aware of where their interests lay, more willing to take action to push them forwards. Then came an abrupt check. The collapse of the July movement sent a wave of demoralisation across proletarian Petrograd. Heady hopes turned to bitter disappointment. Confidence was replaced by cynicism. Angry reproach fell upon those who had done most to raise expectations: the Bolsheviks. The Great Lie – that German gold funded Lenin's party – found a ready audience among a mass movement retreating in confusion.

The lie was fabricated from the most pitiful material. The unsubstantiated testimonies of a minor military agent and a shady businessman were fanned by the liberal-bourgeois media into a great storm of slander, abuse, and vilification.[1] As the lie percolated through the pores of Russian society, meetings of workers and soldiers shouted down Bolshevik speakers; in places, party members felt physically threatened and withdrew from the Soviets altogether. 'The July events', wrote Shlyapnikov,

and the whole accompanying campaign of violence and slander against our organisation interrupted that growth of our influence, which, by the beginning of July, had reached enormous proportions ... The very party became semi-illegal, and had to wage a defensive struggle, relying in the main upon the trade unions and the shop and factory committees.[2]

Recruitment dried up. Some members abandoned the party. The rest kept their heads down. A few were gnawed by doubt. 'I will never forget', wrote the Moscow worker Ratekhin,

one mortally hard moment. A plenary session was assembling [of the district Soviet] ... I saw there were none too many of our Bolshevik comrades ... Steklov, one of the energetic comrades, came right up close to me and, barely

1.   Trotsky 1932–3/1977, 597–60.
2.   Trotsky 1932–3/1977, 758.

enunciating the words, asked: 'Is it true they brought Lenin and Zinoviev in a sealed train? Is it true they are working on German money?'[3]

The Reformist leaders suspected the allegations were false. But most said little or nothing, for the storm promised to sweep back their revolutionary rivals. Kerensky seized the moment to attempt a killer blow. Orders for the arrest of Lenin, Zinoviev, and other Bolshevik leaders were issued on 19 July. 'Now they will shoot us all', Lenin had told Trotsky the day before. 'For them it is the best moment.' The Bolshevik leaders were forced into hiding, justifying their action on the grounds that 'there are no guarantees of a fair trial in Russia at the present moment', and that 'all accusations against us are a simple episode of civil war'.[4]

This was the right decision. Lenin might well have been murdered, and anyway, in prison he would have been rendered powerless. But the decision was controversial. It seemed to imply guilt.[5] Trotsky – who insisted that his name be added to the list of the accused – and other revolutionary leaders were in fact taken into custody.

The police, meantime, launched attacks on the wider mass movement. Some of the more revolutionary regiments were broken up or sent to the front. Arms searches were carried out in the factories and Red Guards disarmed. Bolshevik newspapers were suppressed; one news vendor was murdered in the street by government soldiers. Kerensky accused Kronstadt of harbouring 'persons ... who, influenced by

3.   Trotsky 1932–3/1977, 760.
4.   Chamberlin 1935/1965, 183.
5.   Trotsky 1932–3/1977, 760.

German agents and provocateurs, have called for actions threatening the Revolution and the security of our country'. Under threat of blockade, Raskolnikov and other Bolshevik sailors surrendered themselves: to have called on their comrades for armed resistance would, in the circumstances, have been too risky.

Among the heaviest of the repressive blows was the restoration of the death penalty at the front.[6] The soldiers were to be driven to fight by fear of the firing squad. The effect of the Great Lie was starkest in the trenches, where military imperatives imposed a politics of extremes. Bolsheviks were purged, army committees ignored, soldiers shot for fraternising. Deserters were herded back to the front following mass round-ups. Mutinous regiments were disarmed. Saluting, drilling, and the untrammelled rule of the officer caste were restored along much of the line. Elite shock battalions of loyalist soldiers were formed: the 'Death Battalions'.[7]

The Great Lie cowed the revolutionary movement and allowed the counter-revolution to rear its head and rally its forces. Trotsky described it thus:

In the assault upon the Bolsheviks, all the ruling forces, the government, the courts, the intelligence service, the staffs, the officialdom, the municipalities, the parties of the soviet majority, their press, their orators, constituted one colossal unit ... The slanders poured down like Niagara. If you take into consideration the setting – the war and the revolution – and the character of the accused – revolutionary leaders of

6. Raskolnikov 1925/1982, 193 and 187–209 passim; Chamberlin 1935/1965, 184–5.

7. Trotsky 1932–3/1977, 763–4.

millions who were conducting their party to the sovereign power – you can say almost without exaggeration that July 1917 was the month of the most gigantic slander in world history.[8]

The Great Lie arose in the context of a great offensive. Kerensky's tour of the army, his hysterical speeches to crowds of soldiers, the flood of official propaganda, the democratic phrases and red flags, the slandering and purging of the Bolsheviks, the suppression of mutinous units, the creation of Death Battalions, the partial restoration of the authority of officers: all this contributed to an upsurge of fighting along the Eastern Front in the summer of 1917. The weary, ragged, sullen *Narod* was being rallied, the country as a whole united, around the flag of 'revolutionary defence'. Kerensky was recasting himself as the heroic champion of a fighting people.

The British and the French had underwritten the offensive by shipping vast quantities of rifles, machine-guns, cannon, and ammunition to Russia. The cannon stood 30 metres apart along 100 kilometres of front when the offensive opened. Never before had the Russians enjoyed a five-to-one advantage in firepower. This was enough to enable them to smash through two or three lines of Austro-Hungarian trenches and open a breach 30 kilometres deep in the enemy line.

Then the Germans rushed in reinforcements and coun-terattacked. As they did so, Russian resistance collapsed. Everywhere, entire units – regiments, divisions, corps, armies – evacuated their positions, went into hiding, retreated headlong. Many did not even await the approach of the enemy; the mere rumour of their coming was sufficient to trigger abandonment

---

8.   Trotsky 1932–3/1977, 622–3.

of the line. Elsewhere, orders to march forwards or mount attacks were debated and rejected; and officers who attempted compulsion were sometimes killed.[9] Brusilov, the Russian commander-in-chief, wailed in desperation: 'It is necessary to restore iron discipline, in the fullest sense of the term ... If we delay even a moment, the Army will perish, Russia will perish, we will sink into infamy.' Kerensky contrasted 'heroes who would selflessly die fulfilling their duty to the Motherland' with those he called 'cowards and traitors'; for the latter he demanded 'the only penalty that could frighten them'.

But where were the loyal units to enforce 'iron discipline' and impose 'the only penalty' to be found? The whole army was infected with mutiny. 'Can we really execute entire divisions?' asked one general. If every insubordinate soldier was brought to trial, 'half the army would end up in Siberia'. The army was being 'destroyed', thought another. There 'remained nothing but human dust', opined a third.[10] A great tide of men flowed away from the war during the summer and autumn of 1917. In its wake came the German juggernaut, rolling forwards, spearheaded by a new class of 'storm-troops', a relentless offensive that would eventually bring the Kaiser's men into Riga on the Baltic on 21 August, a mere 300 miles from Petrograd.

Kerensky had failed. The Provisional Government had proved hollow. The revolution was destroying Russia. The country was being wrecked by a compound of military defeat, economic collapse, and social breakdown. The need was of a saviour, a strongman, a leader who would restore order, safeguard property, and repel the invader. So thought

9.   Stone 1969/1971, 2448–53.
10. Lincoln 1986, 356–7, 408–11.

aristocratic and bourgeois Russia. And when Kerensky sacked Alexei Brusilov and replaced him as army commander-in-chief with Lavr Kornilov, a Siberian Cossack general with a bodyguard of machine-gun toting Turcoman warriors, it seemed to many that just such a man had emerged.

The Kornilov Coup

The saviour made a grand appearance in Moscow on 14 August. The occasion was a session of the State Conference, an assembly of 2,414 delegates representing the former Tsarist Dumas, the co-operatives, the trade unions, the banks and big business, the municipalities, and the Soviets. Because it was Kerensky's attempt to create a political base for the new Provisional Government, it was heavily skewed in favour of the Right and private property. The Conference was boycotted by the Bolsheviks as a gerrymandered assembly of counter-revolutionary forces. The Moscow workers greeted it with a 400,000-strong protest strike on the day of its opening.[11] Held in the magnificent surroundings of a grand opera house and intended as a display of national unity, it was in fact a comic-opera prefiguring of the coming civil war. Figures of the Tsarist *ancien regime* formed the Right. The leaders of the Reformist parties formed 'the Left'. The vast crowds of proletarian strikers outside on the first day – massed under banners bearing Bolshevik slogans – represented the revolutionary *Narod*. Agreement was impossible; for much of the time the Conference was consumed by stormy altercation. Kerensky was revealed as the indispensable pivot connecting the two sides. All politics must be personified. The politics

11. Trotsky 1932–3/1977, 658–9.

of impasse – of irreconcilable class contradictions – may find expression in a buffoon. Such was Kerensky: vain, pompous, self-important, his histrionic rhetoric cover for lack of real substance and the hopelessness of the political situation. The impasse became obvious with the arrival of Kornilov.

At the first sitting of the Conference, Kerensky had been given a standing ovation by the Lefts, while the Rights had remained seated. At the second sitting, Kornilov received a standing ovation from the Rights, and the Lefts remained seated.[12] Kornilov had arrived in Moscow to cheering crowds. Richly dressed women had strewn his path with flowers. 'You are the symbol of our unity', proclaimed one Cadet politician. 'Save Russia and a grateful people will crown you.' Ascending the podium, Kornilov told the State Conference that

> the Army must be restored at all costs, for without a recon-structed Army, there can be no free Russia and no salvation of our homeland … Only an Army welded together by iron discipline, only an Army led by the unified will of its leaders can achieve victory … We cannot afford to waste time. Not even a single minute can be wasted.[13]

The 'restoration' of the army was already under way. After his appointment, Kornilov had begun issuing demands of the government: that politicians should not interfere with his military arrangements; that the death penalty should be reintroduced in the rear as well as at the front; that the railways and war industries should be militarised. At the same time, counter-revolutionary forces began to gravitate upon

12.   Trotsky 1932–3/1977, 672–3.
13.   Lincoln 1986, 416–17.

Kornilov's headquarters: the Death Battalions (including women's battalions); the Cavaliers of St George (decorated veterans); the League of Officers; the *Junkers* (as officer cadets were known); and the Council of the Union of Cossacks. The commander-in-chief also summoned the 3rd Cavalry Corps, which included the notorious 'Savage Division' of Caucasian horsemen – not to the front, but to the rear, directing it towards Petrograd. 'Kornilov became a banner', reported General Denikin. 'For some of counter-revolution, for others of the salvation of the Motherland.'[14]

Kerensky was party to the conspiracy. In this he mixed counter-revolutionary malice with political stupidity. He expected to implement Kornilov's programme himself, but was aware that it could not be done without the destruction of the revolutionary movement in the capital. Accordingly, his intention was to provoke the Bolsheviks into calling the workers onto the streets, and to be ready to smash them with loyalist troops. For this purpose, he asked Kornilov to send a cavalry corps to the capital. As the agent detailed to convey this request later explained, the mission was 'To get from General Kornilov a cavalry corps for the actual inauguration of martial law in Petrograd and for the defence of the Provisional Government against any attempt whatever, in particular an attempt of the Bolsheviks.'[15]

Kerensky was a Kornilovist; but, as the Menshevik Sukhanov put it, 'only on the condition that he himself should stand at the head of the Kornilovists'. The plot in which he was engaged was, as Trotsky explained, Byzantine in its duplicity:

---

14.   Chamberlin 1935/1965, 194–9.
15.   Trotsky 1932–3/1977, 704–6.

the Minister-President, without the knowledge of a part of his own Government, behind the back of the Soviets that had given him power, in secrecy from the party of which he was a member, had entered into agreement with the highest generals of the Army for a radical change in the state regime with the help of the armed forces.[16]

But this plan for a military coup – a plan to destroy Red Petrograd with grenades, shootings, and the gallows – was, on Kerensky's part, the act of a political imbecile. Once unleashed, the counter-revolution would be sure to destroy not only the Bolsheviks, but also the Soviets (which the Bolsheviks increasingly dominated), thus collapsing the entire dual-power regime that was the basis of Kerensky's premiership. Not until the very last moment did the truth dawn on the middle-class lawyer whom history had elevated to such heady heights. Last-minute negotiations between Kerensky and Kornilov yielded a peremptory demand from the Tsarist general for a declaration of martial law in Petrograd, the surrendering of all power in the capital to the military, and the resignation *en masse* of the Provisional Government. The Prime Minister was invited to come to the *Stavka* (military headquarters) for his own safety. It was suggested he might be Minister of Justice in a new government.[17]

The conspiracy fell apart. Kornilov had revealed himself as a rival for supreme power. Kerensky promptly cabled the commander-in-chief ordering him to surrender his office, then a further instruction ordering a halt to all troop movements towards Petrograd. Kornilov ignored both. He was

---

16. Trotsky 1932–3/1977, 706–7.
17. Chamberlin 1935/1965, 209–11.

henceforward engaged in an open military coup against the Provisional Government. The revolution faced its most clear and present danger since the February Days. In the judgement of Prince Trubetskoy, head of the *Stavka* diplomatic corps, 'The whole commanding staff, the overwhelming majority of the officers, and the best fighting units of the Army are for Kornilov. On his side in the rear are all the Cossacks, the majority of the military training-schools, and also the best fighting units.'[18]

The Provisional Government had already ceased to function. The Cadet ministers had resigned their offices and disappeared from view: the counter-revolution was now represented by a Cossack general, so there was nothing for the frock-coats to do but await the outcome. The Reformist ministers remained, but it hardly mattered: they commanded no forces, so were powerless. News of the coup became widely known in Petrograd on the night of 27/28 August. The Russian Stock Exchange greeted the approach of Kornilov's Cossack and Caucasian cavalry with a surge in share values.[19] The propertied classes were banking on a prompt termination of the revolution.

The Soviets, on the other hand, even under Reformist leadership, had suddenly awakened to the fact that their very existence was in mortal danger. On the evening of 27 August, a joint session of both Executive Committees – that of the workers and soldiers, and that of the peasants – had agreed to create a new body, a Committee for Struggle with Counter-Revolution, formed of three representatives of each of the main Soviet parties, the Mensheviks, the

18.   Chamberlin 1935/1965, 212–13.
19.   Trotsky 1932–3/1977, 722–3.

Social-Revolutionaries, and the Bolsheviks. This body issued an immediate call for all-out armed resistance to Kornilov.[20]

Why had the Bolsheviks joined the Committee for Struggle with Counter-Revolution? The Provisional Government, which included both Mensheviks and Social-Revolutionaries, had hounded the Bolshevik Party into semi-underground existence, imprisoning or forcing into hiding its leaders, shutting down its newspapers, smearing its members as accomplices of the Kaiser. Kerensky was a reactionary masquerading as a democrat. The Winter Palace and the *Stavka* were twin centres of counter-revolution. What was it that Lenin had said after the July Days? That Kerensky's cabinet was 'Bonapartist' in character and dependent for its existence upon 'a military clique'.[21] The term 'Bonapartist' implied an authoritarian government elevated above society and balanced between two opposing social forces. Lenin's argument was that Kerensky was an embryonic Bonapartist, in that he straddled the division between bourgeoisie and Soviet, but, lacking an army of his own, was compelled to seek an alliance with the generals.

The breach between Kerensky and Kornilov transformed the situation. It was a 'sharp turn' that demanded 'revision and change of tactics'. The main enemy was now Kornilov, because he represented the mailed fist: the crisis had become an open struggle between the army and the Soviets, between armed counter-revolution and the Petrograd proletariat.[22] The argument was carefully nuanced. When Kronstadt sailors asked Trotsky, 'Isn't it time to arrest the Government?', he

---

20.   Chamberlin 1935/1965, 217.

21.   Cliff 1976, 287.

22.   Cliff 1976, 298–301.

answered, 'No, not yet. Use Kerensky as a gun-rest to shoot Kornilov. Afterwards we will settle with Kerensky.'[23] This was the tactic of the united front in action: unity of the working class – Mensheviks, Social-Revolutionaries, and Bolsheviks – to defend the revolution against the immediate and most dangerous enemy. But this, for Lenin, did not mean an alliance with Kerensky: 'We will fight, we are fighting against Kornilov, but we are not supporting Kerensky, but exposing his weakness … In fighting Kornilov, the proletariat will fight not for the dictatorship of Kerensky, but for all the conquests of the Revolution.'[24]

In truth, as in all the great days of the revolution, as in February, April, and July, no call from above was required: tens of thousands of activists embedded in Petrograd's revolutionary mass movement were already in action. The Soviets, in decay for two months under their insipid leadership, suddenly burst back into life, nourished by an upsurge of activity from below, as the workers and soldiers flowed into packed meetings. The Red Guards, suppressed after the July Days, were reborn, with queues of young workers forming to sign up and collect rifles; the proletarian militia was soon 40,000 strong. The giant Putilov works became the centre of resistance in the Peterhof District: the Factory Committee remained in permanent session, new fighting detachments were formed, and workers toiled 16 hours a day to manufacture 100 cannon for the defence of the revolutionary capital. The rail workers – threatened by Kornilov with martial law – tore up track, built barricades, refused to move troop trains, shunted others into sidings. The postal and telegraph clerks refused to transmit

23.   Trotsky 1932–3/1977, 738–9.
24.   Trotsky 1932–3/1977, 821.

military messages. 'The generals', commented Trotsky, 'had been accustomed during the years of war to think of transport and communications as technical questions. They found out now that these were political questions.' Other unions provided funds, offices, transport, and printing-presses to aid the defence.[25]

In the end, it was almost bloodless. The counter-revolutionary forces in the rear were easily cowed. A military commandant in communication with Kornilov was shot by the Kronstadt sailors. Four officers of the Baltic Fleet who refused to swear allegiance to the revolution were also executed. Most of the rest, the secret Kornilovists in Petrograd and elsewhere, went to ground, awaiting the arrival of the Cossacks and Caucasians. But they never came. Trotsky recalled how the army of counter-revolution was immobilised or diverted to the back of beyond by the rail workers:

In a mysterious way, echelons would find themselves moving on the wrong roads. Regiments would arrive in the wrong direction, artillery would be sent up a blind alley, staffs would get out of communication with their units. All the big stations had their own soviets, their railway workers, and their military committees. The telegraphers kept them informed of all events, all movements, all changes ... Parts of the army of Krymov [Kornilov's field commander] were in this way scattered about in the stations, sidings, and branch lines of eight different railways. If you follow on the map the fate of the Kornilov echelons, you get the impression that

25. Trotsky 1932–3/1977, 734–7.

the conspirators were playing at blind-man's-buff on the railway lines.[26]

At the same time, the rank-and-file soldiers were swamped by revolutionary crowds, fraternising, leafleting, arguing, attempting to dissolve a mortal physical threat with the acid of a moral power. The Cossacks were surrounded by 20,000 armed soldiers at Luga. They were given leaflets informing them that Kornilov was an outlaw. The Cossacks held their own meetings. Had they been deceived? Had their officers lied? A delegation of Muslim revolutionaries went to meet their co-religionists of the Savage Division. It included the grandson of a famous hero who had defended the mountains against Tsarism. What was the result? The Caucasians stuck a red flag inscribed 'Land and Freedom' on their commander's staff car.[27]

Thus did the Kornilov Coup boil up, surge forwards, and then melt away into the ground, its high command unable to direct it, its troop trains shunted into nowhere, its soldiery sucked into a revolutionary mass that rose up all around it.

Not only that. The August Days had exposed the violence of the propertied classes, their irreconcilable hatred of the revolution, the impossibility of compromise. They also laid bare the powerlessness of the Provisional Government and the treachery of Kerensky and the Reformist leaders. Not least, they revealed the Bolsheviks to be the most resolute champions of the revolution and of the common people's demands for peace, land, and freedom.

---

26. Trotsky 1932–3/1977, 744–5.
27. Trotsky 1932–3/1977, 741–3.

As the counter-revolution's attempt to solve the national crisis with a Cossack army crumbled to pieces, the mood of Russia's dark masses, shifting only slowly since the July debacle, swung suddenly and sharply to the left. A revolution, Marx once said, needs from time to time the whip of counter-revolution. So it was on this occasion: Kornilov had roused the masses from their slumber, and now – more experienced, more serious, more committed to the party that was truly their own – they were set to rise in unvanquishable number to sweep the landlords, profiteers, and generals of Old Russia into oblivion.

CHAPTER EIGHT

The October Days

The October Days. A still from Soviet filmmaker Sergei Eisenstein's depiction of the storming of the Winter Palace.

Revolution from below

The events in Petrograd during 1917 were underpinned by an escalating land-war in the Russian countryside. The peasants outnumbered the workers more than five to one. Peasant conscripts had shot down striking workers and crushed the urban revolutionary movement in 1905. They would have done so again had the revolution not spread to the countryside in 1917.

The Provisional Government tried to prevent this happening by opposing all direct action by peasants; the official line was that the villages should wait for the Constituent Assembly to decide the land question. All major parties were committed to an elected Constituent Assembly which would frame a new constitution for Russia. What is quite clear is that had the peasants waited, they would never have got the land. The banks had lent the landlords four billion roubles.[1] This commercial alliance between the bourgeoisie and the aristocracy could not be broken without revolutionary action from below. The Reformists (who would dominate the Constituent Assembly when it finally met in January 1918) certainly had no intention of challenging the rights of property from above. On 21 September, for example, Kerensky issued an order forbidding the peasants from taking land, cattle, machinery, or firewood belonging to the big estate-owners; dire penalties were threatened.

But this had no more effect than countless similar injunctions. The repressive apparatus to enforce such government diktats no longer existed. The peasant movement grew and grew: 34 counties had been effected in March, 174 in April, 236 in May,

---

1.   Trotsky 1932–3/1977, 872.

280 in June, and 325 in July.[2] If the movement faltered a little in some areas during the summer, it was only for the action to spread to previously passive regions, and then for the entire land-war to flare up across the whole country in the autumn, with 30 per cent more recorded incidents in September than August, and 43 per cent more in October than September.[3]

At the same time, the struggle became more radical, with the most destitute peasants moving into the front rank, alongside growing numbers of 'self-demobilised' soldiers returning from the front. They were encouraged by the urban workers, many of whom retained strong links with the villages from which they had migrated, often expressed through membership of 'back-home' clubs. The soldiers knew how to fight and were habituated to violence. Again and again, they led the people of their villages into action. 'More and more soldiers came to us from the towns and from the trenches, some of them wounded, some of them demobilised', recalled one peasant villager. 'They brought more news and stirred up the revolutionary sentiment of the peasantry.'[4]

The peasants rolled into action in the manner of all the great land-wars of the past. Manor houses were looted and burned. Grain was seized and livestock driven off. Farm machines and tools were carried away. Whatever could not be taken was smashed. The struggle for the forests was especially bitter – timber for building and firewood for heating were basic needs in the villages – and so was the struggle for grain, especially among the poorest, feeling the pinch of hunger as winter approached in crisis-wracked Russia. The landlords and their

---

2.   Chamberlin 1935/1965, 251.

3.   Trotsky 1932–3/1977, 862–3.

4.   Trotsky 1932–3/1977, 873–4; Chamberlin 1935/1965, 250–3.

agents fled, the authorities lacked the means to restore order, and the villages set about the 'Black Partition' of which they had dreamed for centuries. Land committees were the primary organs of the peasant revolution, but when the militancy of the masses outran what their Social-Revolutionary leaders were prepared to sanction, even the land committees might be superseded by the primitive peasant democracy and direct action of the *mir*, the village commune. The revolution in the countryside – like the revolution in the cities and at the front – found the channels it needed; the flood could not be stemmed.

The general result was a great levelling of land ownership. Poor and landless peasants received sizeable allotments. The middle peasants usually gained something. The rich peasants were often pulled down a peg. The noble estate ceased to exist.[5] Thus was the peasant revolution accomplished from below before it could be authorised from above. Thus, too, was the ground beneath the feet of the counter-revolution turned to quicksand. Trotsky was unequivocal about the world-historic significance of the land-war in the Russian countryside in 1917:

As air currents carry seeds, the whirlwinds of the revolution scattered the ideas of Lenin … The peasantry pushed the Bolsheviks toward power with their revolt. But only after conquering power could the Bolsheviks win over the peasantry, converting their agrarian revolution into the laws of a workers' state … In order that the peasant might clear and fence the land, the worker had to stand at the head

5.   Chamberlin 1935/1965, 256.

of the state: that is the simplest formula for the October Revolution.[6]

In many places, the war against the landlord fused with a war against the national oppressor. Only 70 million of the Tsarist Empire's inhabitants were 'Great' Russians (as opposed to 'Little' Russians or Ukrainians); the remaining 90 million belonged to a national minority. The latter included western peoples like the Finns, Estonians, Latvians, Lithuanians, Poles, and Ukrainians, and eastern peoples like the Muslim Turks of Central Asia. The politics of class and nation were woven into a sociological tapestry of exceptional complexity; but often enough the lines of class antagonism were also those of national resistance, most obviously where native peasants lived under alien landlords. The Bolshevik policy was simple: with the exploited against the exploiter, with the oppressed against the oppressor; above all, opposition to the dominant Great Russian chauvinism of the Tsarist state. In consequence, many national minorities rallied to Lenin's party, often moving into the front line. The crack regiments of Lettish sharpshooters are a notable example. Recruited from Lettish peasants and labourers in the Baltic states, they hated their ancestral Germanic landlords and their Great Russian officers in roughly equal measure. They would play a leading role in the October Insurrection.[7]

The national question preoccupied half the Tsar's soldiers, the land question virtually all of them. Then there was the unrelenting misery of the trenches. The war had taken half the younger able-bodied males from the villages: a vast cull of the

---

6. Trotsky 1932–3/1977, 877–88 passim.
7. Trotsky 1932–3/1977, passim.

Russian peasantry in the service of empire. Millions were dead or maimed. Millions were still rotting at the front in patched coats and leaking boots – sullen, inert, mutinous. Millions more were hiding in the woods or trekking home. In the wake of the Kornilov Coup, the influence of the Bolshevik Military Organisation among the soldiers soared. Even in July, it had boasted 26,000 members organised in 60 branches. Its advance thereafter was unstoppable. One astute observer delivered this gloomy report on the effects of the Kornilov adventure:

> The authority of the commanders was destroyed once and for all. The masses of the soldiers, seeing how a general, a commander-in-chief, had gone against the Revolution, felt themselves surrounded by treason on all sides and saw in every man who wore epaulettes a traitor. And whoever tried to argue against this feeling also seemed a traitor.[8]

Trenches were decorated with white flags to show that no aggressive action would be taken. Officers who attempted to enforce discipline were ignored and sometimes killed. There was an epidemic of 'fragging' – throwing grenades into officer's quarters to take out unpopular occupants. Only the elected soldiers' committees were obeyed. Entire regiments worked out plans for mass departure from the front. Vehicles and trains were commandeered as transport.

The radicalisation was uneven. The troops on the south-western front were far behind those stationed near Petrograd. The Black Sea Fleet was behind the Baltic Fleet. Infantry tended to be ahead of artillerymen, cavalrymen, and the technical branches. The men in the trenches would

8.   Chamberlin 1935/1965, 236–7.

sometimes find it necessary to threaten to bayonet the gunners if they opened fire (and thus provoked enemy retaliation), or they would deliberately cut telephone wires to prevent spotters communicating with their batteries.[9] But if the soldiers were moving at different speeds, they were moving in the same direction: towards an abandonment of the war at the front in favour of the revolution at home. Quite simply, if Russia in 1917 was experiencing the biggest peasant land-war in history – a mass movement of 100 million villagers – it was also experiencing the biggest military mutiny in history – a movement of 10 million soldiers.

The swing to the Bolsheviks among the soldiers was especially sharp in the capital after the Kornilov Coup, when the government again threatened to move garrison units to the front. The strength of this swing was the reason that a Menshevik decision to set up a 'Committee of Defence' backfired. Formed initially of representatives of each of the three main Soviet parties – and shortly renamed the 'Military Revolutionary Committee' (MRC) – it became an expression of the growing radicalism of the soldiers and was destined to operate as the high command of the coming October Insurrection.[10] The Soldiers' Section of the Petrograd Soviet voted on 13 October, by a majority of 283 to 1, to obey only orders endorsed by the MRC. The meaning was clear: control of the Petrograd garrison had passed from the generals to the people. Other signals of the mood in the barracks were equally clear.

Across Russia, power was devolving from higher democratic bodies to lower ones, closer to the people, more directly representative, better able to give immediate expression to the

9.   Chamberlin 1935/1965, 224–35 passim.
10.   Trotsky 1932–3/1977, 941–2.

evolving popular will. Among the workers, power was shifting from the Soviets to factory committees; among the peasants, from the land committees to village communes; and among the soldiers, from the Soviets to regimental committees. The regimental committees in the capital now came together as the Garrison Conference, meeting for the first time on 18 October. The overwhelming majority of regiments now favoured a 'coming-out': an armed urban insurrection, a second revolution, to terminate the threat of counter-revolution and place power in the hands of the people. The roll-call of those who declared themselves ready to go onto the streets at a call from the Petrograd Soviet constituted a majority; most of the rest were neutral; the hostile were so few they were denied the floor.[11]

Even so, it was the workers who were decisive. The peasants could burn the local manor house and divide up the land, but that was only a village revolution. The soldiers could shoot their officer and 'self-demobilise', but even the garrison regiments in the capital were only temporary sojourners – peasants in uniform, weary of war and sick for home. The soldiers did not constitute an urban vanguard. Few had any appetite for fighting, whether at the front or in the streets. Most now followed the Soviets, sympathised with the Bolsheviks, and favoured a coming-out; but equally, they expected others to decide and to act. 'The political condition of the garrison', explained Trotsky, the main organiser and leader of the October Insurrection, 'was thus exceptionally favourable for an insurrection. But its fighting weight was not large....'[12]

11.   Trotsky 1932–3/1977, 947–55.
12.   Trotsky 1932–3/1977, 1032–3.

It was otherwise with the sailors of the Kronstadt naval base and the Baltic Fleet more generally: as a species of skilled worker in uniform, concentrated in large workplaces, they combined 'proletarian resolution with strict military training'.[13] But they were too few in number to take power in a major modern city. The workers, on the other hand, combined revolutionary determination with vast numbers. Their military arm – the Red Guards, organised in factory contingents, perhaps 25,000 in all – would provide the bulk of the fighting forces of the October Insurrection.

Right-wing historians often describe October as a Bolshevik 'coup' made possible by the 'anarchy' into which Russia had fallen by autumn 1917. The misunderstanding is profound. Their basic error is to view history from above, not below. What looks to them like 'anarchy' was, in fact, the leaching away of state authority and the rise of new organs of popular power. What they describe as a 'coup' was, in fact, an expression of the democratic will of millions of workers, soldiers, sailors, and peasants. The Tsarist monarchy had commanded an army of millions. Yet it was overthrown in the February Revolution. The Provisional Government had inherited that army of millions. Yet it was swept away by the October Insurrection. Historical events of this magnitude are not brought about by mere 'coups'. The very success of the October Insurrection hides its true character. The revolution was so ripe – the social crisis so deep, the authority of the government so hollowed out, the masses so willing to support decisive action – that, in the event, a few tens of thousands were sufficient to execute the popular will.

13.   Trotsky 1932–3/1977, 1070.

The Petrograd workers had reached this point as early as July. Held back by a party that feared a re-run of 1905, their confidence had been shaken and they had retreated a distance. But Kornilov had roused them again, and this time, with the rest of Russia fast catching up, there was to be no relapse. At an early morning session of the Petrograd Soviet on 1 September, the Reformists were overturned and the Bolshevik resolution for a government of workers and peasants was passed two to one. The following day, the Finland Soviets voted the same way (700 for, 13 against). Three days later, Moscow (355 to 254). Three days after that, Kiev (130 to 66). And so it continued: September was the month that the Soviets went Bolshevik across Russia.[14]

It amounted to a national referendum on the form of government – whether it should be Provisional or Soviet, parliamentary or popular – and that meant a referendum on which class should rule, the bourgeoisie or the proletariat. But this was not like other referenda – manipulation of a passive electorate by a political elite and its media echo-chambers. This was opinion created from below, by the masses in action, through the living experience of the class struggle, and then formalised in the decisions of countless participatory popular assemblies.

The factory-committee movement in Petrograd was one measure of the depth of the social earthquake reflected in the Bolshevik advance. Because the higher Soviet bodies lagged behind the popular mood, because the Reformist leaderships became a barrier to revolutionary advance, the workers increasingly put their trust in their own factory committees, which were directly and immediately accountable to the

---

14. Trotsky 1932–3/1977, 805–6.

shop-floor. These had emerged in the wake of the February Days to challenge the tyranny of the bosses in the factories. They had launched the fight for the eight-hour day in March. They had held their First Conference in the capital at the end of May, with 570 delegates representing 236 factories employing 337,000 workers; and the Conference had voted overwhelmingly for a Bolshevik resolution demanding workers' control of industry. The Second Conference of Factory Committees of Petrograd and its Environs in August elaborated on this aim:

> It was the duty of the factory committee to ... work out the rules of internal order – the organisation of working time, wages, the hiring and firing and leave of workers and employees, etc. ... [They should have] control over the composition of the administration, and over the dismissal of the members of the administration who cannot guarantee normal relations with the workers, or who are incompetent for other reasons ... All members of the factory administration can enter into service only with the consent of the factory committee.[15]

Top-down management, in short, was to be abolished. Henceforward, there would be white-collar administrators and specialists accountable to the workplace collective, not to the bosses. The drive for control was both defensive – a response to lockouts and sabotage of production by management in the service of the counter-revolution – and offensive – a pushing back of 'the frontier of control' by an increasingly well-organised and class-conscious working class reaching towards people power. Factory committees and workers'

---

15. Cliff 1976, 227–32.

control were the proletarian revolution turned into a practical programme for every factory.[16]

The factory committees became a national movement. An All-Russian Conference of Factory Committees met in Petrograd from 17 to 22 October. A majority of the 167 delegates were Bolsheviks. Trotsky regarded the Conference as 'the most direct and indubitable representation of the proletariat in the whole country'. His speech to the factory delegates was an unequivocal call to insurrection:

> The proletariat must seize power. The army, the peasantry, and the navy all look to it with hope. And your organisation, the factory committees, must become the champions of this idea. At the forthcoming Congress of Soviets the questions of power, of peace, of land – all will be put point-blank. And when the Soviet gives the word, you in the localities must reply, 'We are here!' Your reply must be a united 'All power to the Soviets!'[17]

The crisis of Bolshevism

The Bolshevik Party had grown exponentially. Membership at the beginning of 1917 had been around 24,000. This grew to 80,000 at the end of April, and then 240,000 at the end of July. The respective figures for Petrograd were 2,000, 16,000, and 36,000. The party's members were overwhelmingly working class. The Reval district, for example, reported 3,182 members in August, of whom 2,926 were workers, 209 soldiers or sailors, and just 47 'intellectuals'. The members were also very young.

---

16. Smith 1983, passim.
17. Cliff 1976, 244–5.

At the Party Congress in July/August 1917, the youngest delegate was 18, the oldest 47, and the average age was 29. Lenin was delighted: 'The young are the only people worth working on', he had written to Inessa Armand, the French-Russian revolutionary socialist and feminist, in February.[18] The influx of new members pushed the party to the left. Young workers, radicalised by the crisis and the revolution, burning with indignation, idealism, and passion for change, were intolerant of party veterans whose long years in the underground had taught lessons in caution. Just as the masses were to the left of the party, so the new members were to the left of the old, and the rank and file to the left of the leaders; and at the highest level, at the furthest remove from the struggle, that is, on the Central Committee of the Bolshevik Party, the conservatism of the Old Guard found its most concentrated expression.

In the middle of September, the Central Committee received a letter from the Bolshevik leader, still in hiding since the July Days. (Lenin's leadership was informal. He had no special position. He was simply one member of the Central Committee. His authority was based on political pre-eminence.) The Bolshevik majority in both the Petrograd and Moscow Soviets proved that 'Our day is come', he wrote. A second revolution, an armed insurrection to overthrow the Provisional Government and seize state power, was the order of the day. 'In this matter it is now impossible to be premature.' The recipients were stunned. The old man had gone mad. He was completely out of touch. Not a single member of the Central Committee supported him. Instead they decided to burn the letter.[19]

---

18.   Cliff 1976, 150–1, 159–62.
19.   Trotsky 1932–3/1977, 978–84.

Lenin's perspective reflected the situation not only in Russia, but worldwide. He saw the workers and peasants of Russia as the vanguard of a conflagration set to sweep across war-ravaged Europe and beyond. 'We stand in the vestibule of the world-wide proletarian revolution', he told his comrades. He knew that timing, in revolution as in war, was decisive. He knew that at the climax of revolution, the masses reach a pitch of hope and expectation, but that this mood is momentary, that it is a feverous state of tension that quickly exhausts itself, and that the masses then drop back into weary resignation, laced with cynicism about all things political, leaving the stage of history clear once again for society's traditional rulers. The willingness of the masses to carry out an insurrection was decisive.

Lenin was never the advocate of a coup. He had opposed an insurrection in the July Days. He had spent time since writing a pamphlet, *State and Revolution*, in which he had revived the Marxist theory of the state in the context of revolution. The existing state, he argued, was a top-down repressive apparatus run by members of the ruling class in the interests of the ruling class. It was bourgeois through and through, and could not be taken over by the workers and used to implement socialism: it had to be smashed and replaced with a new kind of bottom-up democratic state. This had been the key lesson of the Paris Commune of 1871:

The Commune … appears to have replaced the smashed state machine 'only' by fuller democracy: abolition of the standing army; all officials to be elected and subject to recall. But as a matter of fact this 'only' signifies a gigantic replacement of certain institutions by other institutions of a fundamentally different type … the abolition of all representation allowances, and of all monetary privileges to officials, the reduction of the remuneration of all servants of the state to the level of workman's wages.[20]

The Soviets and other democratic assemblies like the factory committees, regimental committees, and village communes were, in combination, the embryo of such a bottom-up state. And the moment had arrived when the masses, having placed all their hopes for a better life in these assemblies of their own making, were prepared to support a decisive blow to invest them with supreme power. But revolution is the most concentrated of collective acts. It requires a brain and a central nervous system to direct and co-ordinate the mass collective action of millions of people organised in thousands of assemblies. Now, at the critical moment, at one of history's greatest turning points, the brain had a seizure.

Lenin was desperate. At the end of September, he broke with his own Central Committee, appealing over their heads to the wider party by sending a public document, *The Crisis is Ripe*, to the Petrograd and Moscow Committees and to the Soviets, now with Bolshevik majorities, in both cities. The Central Committee was openly charged with *opposing* an immediate seizure of power. 'That tendency', he continued,

> must be overcome. Otherwise, the Bolsheviks will cover themselves with eternal shame and destroy themselves as a party. For to miss such a moment and 'wait' for the Congress of Soviets would be utter idiocy, or sheer treachery … for it

20. Cliff 1976, 315–22.

would mean losing weeks at a time when weeks and even days may decide everything.[21]

The Bolshevik leader was tireless, sending out a stream of articles, motions, and letters, attempting to stir up the party rank and file against 'the upper circles of the party', where 'a wavering is to be observed, a sort of dread of the struggle for power, an inclination to replace this struggle with resolutions, protests, and conferences'. This was effective. The Kiev Bolsheviks voted by an overwhelming majority against their own 'anti-Leninist' committee. Moscow issued a bitter denunciation of the Central Committee and demanded that it 'take a clear and definite course toward insurrection'. Finally, on 10 October 1917, the Central Committee assembled for its most momentous meeting. Lenin arrived in disguise, in wig and spectacles, and without beard. They met in secret, in the apartment of leading Menshevik Sukhanov, whose Bolshevik wife had made sure her husband would be away that evening. Twelve of the 21 Central Committee members were present. The session lasted ten hours – deep into the night – the Bolshevik leaders sustained by tea with bread and sausage. The resolution committing the Bolshevik Party to the October Insurrection was scribbled hastily by Lenin with the chewed end of a pencil on a sheet of paper taken from a child's notebook:

The Central Committee recognises that both the international situation of the Russian Revolution ... and the military situation ... all this in connection with the peasant insurrection and the swing of popular confidence to our

21. Cliff 1976, 344–5.

party ... and finally the obvious preparation for a second Kornilov attack ... all this places armed insurrection on the order of the day. Thus recognising that the armed insurrection is inevitable and fully ripe, the Central Committee recommends to all organisations of the party that they be guided by this, and from this point of view consider and decide all practical questions.[22]

The vote, when it came, was ten to two. A decisive majority? Not at all: the majority had been pressured from within the party and then browbeaten by Lenin during an all-night session. So even now, two weeks before the October Insurrection, the inner-party struggle continued. The opposition rallied around the two CC dissidents, Grigori Zinoviev and Lev Kamenev, who had immediately issued a party statement arguing that 'to proclaim an armed insurrection now is to put at stake not only the fate of our party but also the fate of the Russian and international revolution'. Their campaign fed the nervousness and hesitation of leading party bodies as they stood on the brink of the ultimate step.

A reconvened Central Committee meeting on 16 October, attended this time by a dozen other leading Bolsheviks, debated at length a proposal that the previous resolution should be taken as a matter of 'general orientation' only, not as an injunction to prepare for immediate armed insurrection. Zinoviev's 'vacillation' motion secured six votes against 15 with three abstentions.

Then, two days later, a bombshell: Zinoviev and Kamenev published an article in Maxim Gorky's Menshevik newspaper *Novaya Zhizn* attacking the whole idea of insurrection. Lenin

22. Trotsky 1932-3/1977, 996–1000.

exploded, denouncing them as 'strike-breakers' and 'blacklegs' and demanding their expulsion from the party. But the two dissidents acted with strong, albeit discreet, support at the highest levels of the party. Joseph Stalin, one of the two editors of *Pravda*, was among the closet oppositionists, responsible for a statement in the party newspaper criticising Lenin's 'sharp tone' and expressing agreement 'in fundamentals' with Zinoviev and Kamenev.[23]

By now, though, the die was cast. The Bolshevik rank and file, embedded in a vast network of popular assemblies, heading up a mass movement throbbing with revolutionary energy, were in motion. And another body – not the wobbling Bolshevik Central Committee – would provide the essential command and control: the Military Revolutionary Committee chaired by Leon Trotsky.

A final comment is in order. The Bolshevik Party – a nationwide network of revolutionary militants rooted in the class struggle of the workers, soldiers, and sailors – was essential to the success of the revolution. This network was the primary transmitter of revolutionary ideas, the primary crucible for the forging of mass leaders, and the primary mechanism for organising united mass action at every level. But it was *not* the 'democratic-centralist' monolith of sectarian myth; it was not a hierarchy in which instructions were handed down from on high to be carried out with military-style discipline by the lower echelons. This is how Trotsky described it:

Between the saints as the Church paints them and the devils as the candidates for sainthood portray them, there are to be found living people. And it is they who make history.

---

23.   Trotsky 1932–3/1977, 1001–14.

The high temper of the Bolshevik Party expressed itself not in the absence of disagreements, waverings, and even quakings, but in the fact that in the most difficult circumstances it gathered itself in good season by means of inner crises, and made good its opportunity to interfere decisively in the course of events. That means that the party as a whole was a quite adequate instrument of revolution.[24]

The October Days

Lenin was right about the timing of insurrection, but wrong about its form. He thought the party might call it in its own name; he was persuaded by Trotsky and others that the Soviets, not the Bolsheviks, should issue the summons to the masses to rise against the Provisional Government.

Lenin was the political genius who built and led the Bolshevik Party. Trotsky was the genius who led the Petrograd Soviet at its decisive hour and who organised the October Insurrection. The Bolshevik Revolution was the achievement of these two political leaders in equal measure. Let the Menshevik Sukhanov stand testimony. In the two weeks after that momentous secret meeting in his own apartment, Sukhanov recalled, Trotsky was a continuous flurry of activity:

He flew from the Obukhov Works to the Fuse Factory, from the Putilov to the Baltic Mills, from the Riding School to the barracks, and it seemed he spoke in all places at the same time. Every Petrograd worker and soldier knew who he was and had heard him speak. His influence – among the masses and at headquarters – was overpowering. During these days,

24. Trotsky 1932–3/1977, 1015–16.

he was the central figure and the real hero of this remarkable page in history.[25]

Lenin, of course, was in hiding all this while, only to emerge on the morrow of victory.

The October Insurrection was a masterpiece in the art of revolution. Delegates to the Second All-Russian Congress of Soviets were arriving in the capital. It was expected to have a Bolshevik and Left Social-Revolutionary majority. But as a large, new, somewhat chaotic mass assembly – finding its way, sorting out procedures, electing administrative bodies, pushing forwards through a thicket of resolutions and speeches – making the decision to launch an armed insurrection, and organising such an enterprise, might have been problematic. The Military Revolutionary Committee, in carrying out the insurrection in the name of the Soviets, was anticipating the will of the Congress. It was acting on the principle that first is the deed. You have to act, because by acting you change reality; and when reality changes, in so far as people welcome the change, they will endorse the decision that brought it about.

Though the 25th of October has been sanctified as the day of the insurrection, it was not in fact the work of a single day. The insurrection began on the 20th and was not completed until the 26th: so it was as much a process as the February Revolution had been. Much of the illusion that it was some sort of coup depends upon this false compression. Trotsky, already Chair of the Petrograd Soviet, became Chair also of the newly formed Military Revolutionary Committee (MRC) on the 20th. Trotsky was unequivocal about the need for this highly centralised directory:

---

25. Lincoln 1986, 433.

> People do not make revolution eagerly any more than they
> do war. A revolution takes place when there is no other way
> out. And the insurrection, which rises above a revolution
> like a peak in the mountain chain of events, can no more
> be evoked at will than revolution as a whole ... Just as a
> blacksmith cannot seize the red-hot iron in his naked hand,
> so the proletariat cannot directly seize power.[26]

His point was that the power of the popular movement had
to be concentrated into a single point, like the tip of a spear;
only thus could the masses achieve what they desired – peace,
bread, and land through the seizure of power by democratic
mass assemblies which were the embodiment of true people
power. And from this moment – irrespective of residual
vacillation by the Bolshevik leadership – the insurrection
had begun. The MRC – which had been boycotted by
the Reformists – was an exclusively Bolshevik and Left
Social-Revolutionary body, committed from the outset to
organising an armed insurrection. MRC 'commissars' were
immediately appointed to all combatant units to ensure full
intelligence, co-ordination, and the carrying out of Soviet
orders. The MRC also established control over the arsenals
and the printing presses. In this, though, and in all matters, it
was assisted by action from below, as, for example, when the
print workers' union informed the MRC of an increase in
Black Hundred leaflets and pamphlets, prompting immediate
action to suppress it.[27]

The following day, 21 October, came the crucial decision of
the Garrison Conference – the great assembly of regimental

---

26. Lincoln 1986, 437.
27. Trotsky 1932–3/1977, 960–2.

committees in the capital – to break with military headquarters and support the armed insurrection. Trotsky proposed three short resolutions: that all steps taken by the MRC be given full support; that there should be 'a peaceful review of forces' the following day; and that 'the All-Russia Congress of Soviets must take power in its hands and guarantee to the people peace, bread, and land'. Hundreds voted in favour, 50 or so abstained, none voted against. 'The noose around the neck of the February regime was being drawn in a reliable knot.'

The 'peaceful review of forces' had been called for 22 October in response to a counter-revolutionary provocation: a proposed Cossack 'religious procession'. The latter was called off – crowded out by the revolutionary upsurge – but the Soviet demonstration went ahead. It took the form of packed mass meetings in every possible auditorium, great and small, across Red Petrograd. The leader of the October Insurrection described it thus:

The people of the slums, of the attics and basements, stood still by the hour in threadbare coat or grey uniform, with caps or heavy shawls on their heads, the mud of the streets soaked through their shoes, an autumn cough catching at their throats. They stood there packed shoulder-to-shoulder, and crowding even closer to make room for more, to make room for all, listening tirelessly, hungrily, passionately, demandingly, fearing lest they miss a word of what it is so necessary to understand, to assimilate, and to do ... The experience of the revolution, the war, the heavy struggle of a whole bitter lifetime, rose from the deeps of memory in each of these poverty-driven men and women, expressing itself in simple and imperious thoughts: this way we can go no further; we must break a road into the future.[28]

No further. A new road. The American journalist and radical John Reed, newly arrived in Petrograd, was witness to this. The city was always bleak in autumn, a place of grey skies, frequent rain, chill winds, long nights, mud everywhere; but to this was added the shortages, the food becoming ever scarcer, the queues longer, the wait for bread, milk, sugar, tobacco sometimes taking hours. The contrast with the rich on the Nevsky Prospect and other fashionable streets was sharper than ever:

Young ladies from the provinces came up to the capital to learn French and cultivate their voices, and the gay, young, beautiful officers wore their gold-trimmed crimson *bashliki* and their elaborate Caucasian swords around the hotel lobbies. The ladies of the minor bureaucratic set took tea with each other in the afternoon, carrying each her little gold or silver or jewelled sugar-box, and half a loaf of bread in her muff, and wished the Tsar were back, or that the Germans would come, or anything that would solve the servant problem.[29]

But Reed saw much more than the polar opposites of class society. He saw the great popular rising from the depths, visible in countless tiny incidents and comments:

---

28. Trotsky 1932–3/1977, 966–8.
29. Reed 1926/1977, 37–9.

We came down to the front of the 12th Army, back of Riga, where gaunt and bootless men sickened in the mud of desperate trenches; and when they saw us they started up, with their pinched faces and the flesh showing blue through their torn clothing, demanding eagerly, 'Did you bring anything to read?'[30]

Despite the privation, the desperate struggle for daily survival, there was an explosion of reading, listening, talking, meeting, debating:

Lectures, debates, speeches – in theatres, circuses, school-houses, clubs, soviet meeting-rooms, union headquarters, barracks … Meetings in the trenches at the front, in village squares, in factories … What a marvellous sight to see … the Putilov factory pour out its 40,000 to listen to Social-Democrats, Socialist-Revolutionaries, Anarchists, anybody, whatever they had to say, as long as they would talk. For months in Petrograd, and all over Russia, every street-corner was a public tribune. In railway trains, street-cars, always the spurting up of impromptu debate, everywhere… [31]

Reed spoke at one of these endless meetings in a giant Petrograd munitions plant:

The meeting took place between the gaunt brick walls of a huge unfinished building, 10,000 black-clothed men and women packed around a scaffolding draped in red, people

30.   Reed 1926/1977, 40.
31.   Reed 1926/1977, 40.

heaped up on piles of lumber and bricks, perched high up on shadowy girders, intent and thunder-voiced. Through the dull, heavy sky now and again burst the sun, flooding reddish light through the skeleton windows upon the mass of simple faces upturned to us.[32]

The day of the 'peaceful review of forces' – a day of mass meetings unprecedented in the history of the world – was the day when these vast masses were 'welded in one gigantic cauldron' (Trotsky's phrase) around the simple, practical, obvious, inescapable Bolshevik programme for the resolution of the social crisis:

All power to the Soviets – both in the capital and in the provinces.
Immediate truce on all fronts. An honest peace between peoples.
Landlord estates – without compensation – to the peasants.
Workers' control over industrial production.
A faithfully and honestly elected Constituent Assembly.[33]

This massive demonstration of Soviet power crowded out the Provisional Government by revealing its isolation and impotence. An MRC resolution the following day sealed the matter, declaring that its commissars were inviolable representatives of the Soviet, and that opposition to them therefore amounted to defiance of Soviet authority. Thus was the rule of the Provisional Government terminated two days before

32. Reed 1926/1977, 52.
33. Reed 1926/1977, 53.

its physical liquidation.[34] This, of course, was merely formal sanction from on high for actual practice on the ground. Everywhere – quietly, easily, without fanfare or drama – power was passing from one class to another, as officers, managers, landlords, and policemen ceased to give orders, and as what Reed called 'the Dark People' of the Soviets assumed control.

So it continued for three days more. Sukhanov, hostile but honest, found the whole process fascinating. He thought that the military operations 'seemed more like a changing of the guard'.[35] John Reed, the drama-hungry journalist, was equally bemused. He witnessed the chaotic bustle, the endless coming and going, at the Smolny Institute, the headquarters of the insurrection, which he saw 'thronged with hurrying shapes of soldiers and workmen, some bent under the weight of huge bundles of newspapers, proclamations, printed propaganda of all sorts'. He forced his way along the corridors, where every room had become the office of a faction, a committee, a bureau, or something to do with the multifarious business of the Soviet. In the downstairs refectory, 'The benches along the wooden tables were packed with hungry proletarians, wolfing their food, plotting, shouting rough jokes across the room.'[36] But in the streets, though he encountered checkpoints with their huddles of soldiers and red militia, he could not find the historic panorama with a cast of thousands that the occasion seemed to require.

On every corner, immense crowds were massed around a core of hot discussion. Pickets of a dozen soldiers with fixed

34.   Trotsky 1932–3/1977, 969–71.

35.   Lincoln 1986, 444.

36.   Reed 1926/1977, 54–5.

bayonets lounged at the street crossings, red-faced old men in rich fur coats shook their fists at them, smartly-dressed women screamed epithets; the soldiers argued feebly, with embarrassed grins.[37]

There were last-minute hitches. The allegiance of the garrison of the Peter and Paul Fortress was uncertain. It stood threateningly on the opposite bank of the Neva from the Winter Palace. It required a personal visit by Trotsky to win the soldiers over. This had the added bonus of the 100,000 rifles held in the fortress's Kronverksky Arsenal. The Peter and Paul Fortress, in the event, became the arsenal of the insurrection: there were soon trucks pulling up from all over Petrograd to secure a stack of rifles. Similar concerns centred on the armoured car division and, finally, on a bicycle battalion. In each case, however, the soldiers were won over without violence.[38] The insurrection found its way by moral power – by the overwhelming pressure of the great mass of democratic opinion organised in the Soviet movement – and has thereby deceived generations of historians into mistaking the greatest popular revolution in history for a military coup. 'It was not necessary to employ force,' explained Trotsky, 'for there was no resistance. The insurrectionary masses lifted their elbows and pushed out the lords of yesterday.'[39]

The way was eased by a pitiful effort at pre-emptive action by the Provisional Government on 24 October. It marshalled its forces: the *Junkers*, the officer-cadets of the military schools; a Women's Shock Battalion; some Cossacks;

37. Reed 1926/1977, 95.

38. Trotsky 1932–3/1977, 959, 970–1, 1062.

39. Trotsky 1932–3/1977, 1073.

an artillery unit; a ragbag of officers who happened to be in the capital. This was supplemented with an appeal to headquarters to send reliable units (as if these existed). There were threats to suppress newspapers, cut telephone lines, remove commissars, and prosecute the Military Revolutionary Committee. None were effective. The Provisional Government was an intelligence without muscles or motor function. But these puny spasms were just enough to convict the government of counter-revolutionary intent and validate the defensive disguise which the insurrection continued to wear. 'The enemy of the people took the offensive during the night', announced the Soviet communiqué. 'The Military Revolutionary Committee is leading the resistance to the assault of the conspirators.'[40]

Smolny was converted into a combined fortress and military headquarters. 'The massive façade of Smolny blazed with lights as we drove up,' recalled Reed,

and from every street converged upon it streams of hurrying shapes dim in the gloom. Automobiles and motor-cycles came and went; an enormous, elephant-coloured armoured automobile, with two red flags flying from the turret, lumbered out with screaming siren ... The canvas covers had been taken off the four rapid-fire guns on each side of the doorway, and the ammunition-belts hung snake-like from their breeches. A dun herd of armoured cars stood under the trees in the courtyard, engines going. The long, bare, dimly illuminated halls roared with the thunder of feet, calling, shouting... [41]

40. Trotsky 1932–3/1977, 1055.
41. Reed 1926/1977, 96.

The MRC commissars completed the takeover of the capital the following day, 25 October, seizing the Electric Power Station, the Main Post Office, the Nikolaevsky Bridge, the State Bank, and the Warsaw Station: all these fell to the insurrectionaries between midnight and dawn. So complete was the victory – so silent and unspectacular – that Kerensky was almost too late to make his escape. He was finally carried from the city huddled in the back of an American Embassy car around noon.[42] By then, the ring of Red Guards and revolutionary soldiers and sailors was drawing tight around the Winter Palace.

On this day, the whole energy of Russia's mighty conflagration had became concentrated in the hands of perhaps 25,000 armed men – workers, soldiers, and sailors. There was little for anyone else to do. Most workers remained at home, most soldiers in their barracks. They had debated, voted, and given their activist vanguard a mandate. Now it was simply a matter of executing the formal transfer of power from one class to another. There was no looting or rioting. Theatres, cinemas, and shops remained open. Normal life continued on the Nevsky, within sight and sound of the desultory siege under way at the Winter Palace.

The climax was anti-climax. The Winter Palace, the seat of government, was held by a motley collection of Tsarist officers, Cossacks, *Junkers*, war veterans, and the Women's Battalion. This was the sum total of social forces prepared to fight for Kerensky (who, in any case, had fled). Threatened from the River Neva by the guns of the battleship *Aurora*, and unable to prevent armed workers and sailors infiltrating the palace's vast

---

42.   Lincoln 1986, 446.

labyrinth of entrances and passageways, the defence crumbled amid frantic scuffles. It would all look far more impressive in Eisenstein's 1928 movie. Trotsky had already reported to the Petrograd Soviet that 'the Provisional Government has ceased to exist'. He was a little premature: the guns were still firing. It was almost two o'clock on the morning of 26 October when Vladimir Antonov-Ovseyenko, a young intellectual with long hair, clipped beard and moustache, wire-rimmed spectacles, and filthy clothes, led his armed detachments into the meeting room of the Provisional Government. 'In the name of the Military Revolutionary Committee,' Antonov-Ovseyenko announced, 'I declare that you – all of you – members of the Provisional Government are under arrest.'[43]

The Second All-Russian Congress of Soviets was in session that morning. Lenin had emerged from hiding to address it. He told the assembled delegates that 'We shall now proceed to construct the socialist order.' The Congress then passed an appeal addressed to 'the workers, soldiers, and peasants' drafted by the Bolshevik leader. It stated:

The Soviet government will propose an immediate democratic peace to all peoples and an immediate armistice on all fronts. It will secure the transfer of the estates of the landlords ... to the control of the peasants' committees, without compensation. It will protect the rights of the soldiers by introducing complete democracy in the army. It will establish workers' control over production. It will see to it that the Constituent Assembly is convened at its appointed time. It will see to it that bread is supplied to the

43.   Lincoln 1986, 448–52.

cities and articles of prime necessity to the villages. It will guarantee all nations inhabiting Russia the genuine right of self-determination.

The Congress decrees: all power in the localities shall pass to the Soviets of Workers', Soldiers', and Peasants' Deputies... [44]

44. Lenin 1917d, 399–400.

PART THREE

The Darkness, 1918–1938

CHAPTER NINE

World Revolution?

Spreading the revolution. German revolutionaries
man the barricades in Berlin in January 1919.

A carnival of the oppressed

The Second All-Russian Congress of Soviets which assembled on 25 October was the 'parliament' of the new revolutionary regime. Because delegates continued to arrive from remote regions, and because party allegiances were sometimes uncertain, we do not have precise figures for the balance of forces. What is clear, however, is that the Bolsheviks were the largest party, with about 60 per cent of the seats, and their Left Social-Revolutionary allies accounted for another 15 per cent or so, giving the Left a thumping majority. The Mensheviks and Right SRs immediately walked out, refusing to recognise the insurrection, leaving only some smaller left groups alongside the Bolsheviks and Left SRs.

The Congress set up a new government, the Council of People's Commissars (the Sovnarkom). This body, which initially numbered 15, was the 'cabinet' of the new regime. The most important members were Lenin, who was Chairman, and Trotsky, who was first Commissar of Foreign Affairs and later Commissar of Army and Navy Affairs.[1]

History records only a few such instances of genuine people power. The new 'ministers' had to hand-write their own decrees for lack of clerical assistants. The new 'cabinet secretary' had to bang out the minutes on a commandeered typewriter with two fingers because there was no typist. The new 'Finance Minister' owed his appointment to the fact that he had once worked as a clerk in a French bank. When the 'War Minister' tried to flag down a car in the street to take him to the front, he was told it belonged to the First Machine-Gun Regiment and he could not have it.[2]

---

1. Trotsky 1932–3/1977, 1148; Cliff 1978, 2–5.
2. Cliff 1978, 6–7, 22.

The new 'parliament' of the revolution seemed equally incongruous when set against the bourgeois assemblies with which it was inevitably compared. The American journalist John Reed was an eyewitness at the Second Soviet Congress. Here, for him, during these 'ten days that shook the world', was the living embodiment of a world turned upside down:

> I stood there watching the new delegates come in – burly, bearded soldiers, workmen in black blouses, a few long-haired peasants. The girl in charge ... smiled contemptuously ... 'See how rough and ignorant they look! The Dark People...' It was true: the depths of Russia had been stirred, and it was the bottom which came uppermost now.[3]

The enemies of the new regime – Monarchists, Liberals, Reformists – were convinced it could not last. On the very day of the insurrection, one conservative daily, looking at the social character of the revolutionary movement through a lens of bourgeois privilege, was sneering about the prospects:

> Let us suppose for a moment that the Bolsheviks do gain the upper hand. Who will govern us then? The cooks perhaps, those connoisseurs of cutlets and beefsteaks? Or maybe the firemen? The stableboys, the chauffeurs? Or perhaps the nursemaids will rush off to meetings of the Council of State between the diaper-washing sessions. Who then? Where are the statesmen? Perhaps the mechanics will run the theatres, the plumbers foreign affairs, the carpenters the post office. Who will it be?[4]

---

3. Cliff 1978, 3.
4. Cliff 1978, 1–2.

History would soon reveal whether 'statesmen' were essential or disposable. Everything depended on the initiative and creativity of the masses. To encourage this, the Sovnarkom issued a string of decrees in rapid succession:

- A decree on peace (26 October) calling upon 'all the belligerent peoples and their governments to start immediate negotiations for a just, democratic peace'.
- A decree on land (26 October) stating that 'private ownership of land shall be abolished forever' and that all land shall 'become the property of the whole people and pass into the use of all those who cultivate it'.
- A decree on the national question (2 November) proclaiming full equality and the right of all peoples to 'free self-determination, up to secession and formation of an independent state'.
- A decree on workers' control (14 November) stipulating that workplaces were to be run by 'all the workers of the given enterprise through their elected bodies' in the context of 'planned regulation of the national economy'.
- A decree on participatory democracy (22 November) arguing that 'the electors' right to recall those elected' was 'the fundamental principle of true democracy ... [in] ... all representative assemblies without exception'.
- Two decrees on the emancipation of women (16 and 18 December) declaring full equality of men and women, making divorce automatic upon request by either spouse, and legitimising children born out of wedlock.

And there were many more over the next three years: a decree abolishing the old judiciary and setting up people's courts; a decree guaranteeing complete religious freedom, but forbidding religious indoctrination in schools; a decree legalising abortion on demand (the first in the world); a decree legalising homosexuality (another first).

But these were not laws to be imposed by police and judges. They were calls to action. 'Decrees are instructions which call for practical work on a mass scale', Lenin told the Eighth Party Congress in March 1919. Like the leaflets of the underground years, the decrees of the revolutionary epoch were agitational. 'The purpose of a decree is to teach practical steps to the hundreds, thousands, and millions of people who heed the voice of the Soviet government', Lenin insisted. 'This is a trial in practical action ...'.[5]

The British journalist Arthur Ransome (later famous as author of *Swallows and Amazons*) knew Russia well. Visiting again in early 1919, he reported on the explosion of creative activity unleashed by the October Revolution. Take education. Where there had been six universities, there were now 16. Attendance was open to all and free. Since the decree abolishing entry qualifications, enrolments at Moscow University had doubled. State funds had been supplied to provide free school meals, and, for children who needed them, free clothes and footwear. Colleges were set up for workers. 'The workmen crowd to these courses', reported Ransome. 'One course, for example, is attended by a thousand men, in spite of the appalling cold of the lecture rooms.' The Commissariat of Public Education was also responsible for libraries. The number of these had doubled in Petrograd and tripled in Moscow since the revolution. In one country district, there were now 73 village libraries, 35 larger libraries, and 500

5. Cliff 1978, 5–11.

hut libraries or reading-rooms. Russia was flooded with printed matter – newspapers, pamphlets, political tracts by Marx, Lenin, and Trotsky, cheap editions of Tolstoy, Dostoevsky, and Turgenev, and much more. Post offices became distribution centres, and bookselling kiosks enjoyed a boom in sales.[6] The workers' state provided the framework for all this activity; but the initiative came from below. A small incident at the beginning of a countrywide literacy programme illustrates this perfectly. Two nurses wrote to Commissar of Public Education, Anatoly Lunacharsky, as follows: 'We know that across the vast expanse of the Russian land there are corners where people have not yet heard the voice of a person who can read and write. That's where we want to go.'[7]

But the odds against the fledging regime were daunting. The cities were gripped by shortages of food and fuel. The collapse in the production of civilian goods during the war and the revolution meant that peasants had nothing to buy and therefore no incentive to sell their foodstuffs. The proletariat and the industrial sector were dwarfed by the vast agrarian hinterland. The revolution faced a 'scissors crisis': unable to supply the industrial centres, it could not produce the goods needed in the countryside, and this led to yet further falls in output – a widening of the gap between town and country, proletarian and peasant. The size of the industrial workforce is one measure of the crisis. It numbered 3.6 million in 1917, 2.5 million in 1918, 1.5 million in 1920, and 1.1 million in 1922. Petrograd in the winter of 1918 was, according to novelist Alexei Tolstoy (a remote relative of Leo), 'starving … bitten through by polar winds, a town without coal and

---

6. Ransome 1919/1992, 149–53.

7. Haynes 2002, 39.

bread, its factory chimneys extinguished, a town like a raw human nerve'.[8] The Bolshevik feminist Alexandra Kollontai, speaking to American journalist Louise Bryant, joked, 'Surely you must understand that there is a great deal of moral satisfaction in deciding whether you want thick cabbage soup or thin cabbage soup.'[9]

Radical idealism and popular enthusiasm could sustain the revolution for a time. But they could not overcome hunger, cold, and disease. Eventually, if the economic crisis was not resolved, if the socialist experiment was not underpinned by material security, the revolution would be consumed by the primeval backwardness of Old Russia. To survive for long, the workers' state needs to break its isolation and gain access to Europe's reserves of industrial power. If, on the other hand, it remained isolated and unaided, it would eventually succumb. Only world revolution could rescue the Bolshevik regime.

A tidal wave of revolution

Capitalism is a world system. For Marx, 'the establishment of modern industry and the world market' went hand in hand. Because industrialisation confers huge commercial advantages, and because goods and services are traded internationally, capitalism imposes itself on a global scale through the imperatives of economic and military competition. The cotton goods of a Manchester textile mill were cheaper than the homespun of an Indian villager even when traded half way round the world. The machine-guns and artillery of European

---

8. Haynes 2002, 50–1.
9. Haynes 2002, 39.

soldiers were capable of destroying armies of native spearmen and musketeers.

If capitalism is a world system, it follows that the working class is an international class. Workers are divided by nation, but nationalism does not reflect their true interest. To take on the bosses, who operate globally, workers have to unite across national boundaries. To achieve emancipation, they have to destroy the bourgeois nation-state and create an alternative workers' state based on direct democracy. To build a socialist economy, they have to take collective control of the workplaces, the transport system, and the global trade networks. To defend their gains and complete their revolution, they have to spread the struggle across the world.

There is no such thing, therefore, as 'socialism in one country'. Marx, Engels, Lenin, Trotsky, and many other leading Marxist thinkers have all stressed that proletarian revolution has to be worldwide or it will fail. A socialist 'siege economy' can only ever be temporary. Eventually, either poverty and insecurity will force the revolution to turn in on itself and create new forms of exploitation in order to survive. Or the workers' state will succumb to hostile pressure – some combination of economic boycott, internal civil war, and foreign military aggression.

This knowledge was fundamental to the thinking of the Bolshevik leaders after the October Insurrection. It was the reason they prioritised the creation of the Communist International (aka the Comintern or Third International) in 1919. The Bolsheviks wanted to create a revolutionary international to replace the Second International of Social Democratic parties which had broken up as its respective constituents voted to back their own governments at the outbreak of the First

World War. The new Comintern was to be the high command of world revolution. The first four congresses were genuinely revolutionary assemblies of growing size and importance. The First Congress (March 1919) comprised 51 delegates from 33 countries, the Fourth (November-December 1922) 408 delegates from 61 countries.[10]

How realistic was the Comintern's attempt to foster world revolution in the years after 1917?

Revolution had broken out in Russia first because it was the weakest of the great powers. But it soon spread. By the third winter of the war, the experience of modern industrialised warfare was imposing massive strain on the whole of European society. With millions dead, millions maimed, millions starving, and millions homeless, a wave of desertion, mutiny, strikes, and demonstrations swept across Europe. Two-thirds of the French army on the Western Front mutinied and refused to mount further attacks. The Italian army fled the battlefield at Caporetto, and tens of thousands threw away their rifles and headed for home singing the *Internationale* and shouting '*Viva Russia!*' From late 1918 onwards, the revolutionary contagion spread through the former Central Powers – through Germany, Austria, Hungary, and Turkey. German sailors mutinied when ordered out to sea and triggered a revolution which ended the war and brought down the Kaiser within a fortnight. By the end of 1918, red flags flew over Berlin, Munich, Vienna, and Budapest. Everywhere, in the forefront of the popular revolt, were soldiers and sailors. Quite literally, millions of men across Europe broke discipline to join mass revolution-

10. Faulkner 2013, 209–10.

ary movements of workers and peasants directed against their own political and military elite.[11]

Germany, the super-state and industrial colossus at the heart of Europe, was the decisive battleground of the world revolution. Germany had lost 1.8 million soldiers in the First World War, while a further 750,000 civilians had died of starvation at home. By the second half of the war, the diet of the average German worker averaged only two-thirds of the calories needed for long-term survival. On 9 November 1918, a revolution started by mutinous sailors in Kiel reached Berlin. Two days before the Armistice on the Western Front, hundreds of thousands were on the streets. The city was awash with red flags and socialist banners. The anti-war revolutionary socialist Karl Liebknecht addressed the crowds from the balcony of the imperial palace and proclaimed a 'socialist republic' and 'world revolution'. The First World War – the bloodiest carnage in human history up to that time – had been ended by the revolutionary action of millions of workers, soldiers, sailors, and peasants across Europe, first on the Eastern Front, now on the Western.

A proletarian insurrection in Germany would have brought the richest industrial economy and the largest working class in Europe over to the side of socialist revolution, bringing immediate succour to the Bolshevik regime in Russia, establishing workers' power from the North Sea to the Pacific, and, in all probability, ensuring that the revolution would go global. Germany's 'November Days' revolution had seen mass demonstrations, mass strikes and mutinies, and the rapid formation of a network of workers', soldiers', and sailors' councils. The Russian Revolution had shown that such a

11.   Faulkner 2013, 202–5.

network represented a potential alternative state structure based on direct democracy. But the German councils chose to hand power to a traditional parliamentary-type government. A new administration formed of reformist ministers was endorsed by an assembly of 1,500 workers' and soldiers' delegates. This event revealed both the strength of the councils – their backing was needed – and the weakness of their politics – they put their trust in professional career politicians. This was a re-run of Russia's February Days translated into German – the creation of a dual-power regime.

On 4 January 1919, the Reformist government sacked Berlin's radical chief of police for refusing to take action against working-class protests. Hundreds of thousands of workers poured onto the streets, many of them armed. An 'Interim Revolutionary Committee' was installed at police headquarters. But the leadership was uncertain, local troops remained hostile, and support for the action outside Berlin was minimal. The Berlin activists had been goaded into action before the revolution had ripened. The revolutionary capital was isolated. Not only the *Freikorps* – fascist-type paramili-taries – but many soldiers from outside Berlin were willing to participate in what turned out to be the bloody suppression of the 'Spartakus Rising'. Karl Liebknecht was knocked unconscious and shot. Rosa Luxemburg's skull was smashed with a rifle butt, she was then shot, and her body was thrown into a canal. The German Revolution had been decapitated.

In the July Days of 1917, the Bolsheviks had reined back the Petrograd proletariat to prevent a premature seizure of power in the capital. In January 1919, the Spartakus League, an embryonic Communist Party, failed to do the same in Berlin – and paid a terrible price.

The setback was not necessarily fatal. The crisis continued to mature across Germany. Support flowed from the moderate SPD to the more radical USP and the revolutionary KPD (the German Communist Party). The *Freikorps* faced increasingly effective resistance from armed workers and revolutionary soldiers. By March 1920, an estimated 20,000 had been killed in a series of regional civil wars. At this point, the German ruling class launched a 'law and order' coup, sending troops into Berlin, overthrowing the SPD government, and appointing a conservative bureaucrat called Kapp in its place.

For Kapp, read Kornilov. And just as in Russia in August 1917, the Right had misjudged the political situation. The head of the main union confederation called a general strike. Millions of workers responded. They also formed new councils and took up arms. The 'Ruhr Red Army' freed Germany's greatest industrial region of all right-wing troops. The 'Kapp Putsch' collapsed in a few days, and the SPD ministers returned to office. The attempted coup had exposed the true nature of the ruling class and the great strength of the working class. The confidence of German workers soared and they moved sharply to the left.

But the potential was not realised. The KPD drew back from proletarian insurrection. The Kapp Putsch did not, like the Kornilov Coup of August 1917, pave the way for socialist revolution. Too bold in January 1919, the KPD leaders had learnt their lesson too well, and now, in wholly different circumstances, proved too timid.

Timing is all in the art of revolution. The summer of 1920 was perhaps a moment when revolutionaries could have led the working class to victory in the heart of Europe. Italy, like Germany, was then on the brink of revolution. The imperialist war had levered open deep fractures in an unstable social order. The country had lost half a million dead in the First World War. The misery of the trenches was matched by bread shortages and hunger on the home front. The ancient poverty of the villages, the new forms of exploitation in the factories of the north, and the carnage and privation of the war combined to produce the *Biennio Rosso* – Italy's 'Two Red Years' of 1919 and 1920.

Summer 1919 saw a three-day general strike in solidarity with the Russian Revolution. Spring 1920 saw Turin metal-workers on strike demanding recognition for their *camere del lavoro* – the 'factory councils' which leading revolutionary Antonio Gramsci saw as the Italian equivalent of Russia's Soviets. The movement peaked in August 1920. Engineering workers in Milan occupied their factories in response to a lockout by the employers. An occupation movement then swept the 'industrial triangle' of north-western Italy. Some 400,000 metal-workers and 100,000 others took part. The occupied factories were treated like military bases. They were defended against the police, and arms were stockpiled inside them. The Italian working class had had enough: the mood among workers was insurrectionary.

The government was paralysed. The Prime Minister admitted to the Senate that he lacked the forces to suppress the movement. So he made some concessions and cut a deal with the union leaders. The Socialist Party was not prepared to challenge this decision. Reformists dominated the apparatus of both unions and party.

Had a large, well-rooted revolutionary party led an insurrection in August 1920, it is likely that the Italian working class could have taken state power and pulled the mass of peasants and the rural and urban poor into action behind it. The primary reason this did not happen was lack of revolutionary leadership, organisation, and will. The price paid was very high. The retreating proletarian movement was soon to be overwhelmed by an advancing fascist one: Mussolini's Blackshirts took power in October 1922.

The convulsions were not restricted to Germany and Italy. They were felt across the whole of Europe and beyond. At the end of 1918, the liberal-nationalist government in Hungary collapsed and was replaced by a radical 'Soviet' government of Communists and Social Democrats led by Bela Kun. In April 1919, a 'Soviet Republic' was also established in Bavaria, and in that same month revolutionaries attempted to seize power in Vienna. A fleeting glimpse was offered of a possible alternative future: Budapest, Bavaria, and Vienna might have formed a revolutionary bloc in the heart of Europe.

It was not to be. In each case, the revolutionaries were not strong enough to prevent reformists from derailing the revolution. One of the Bavarian revolutionary leaders, facing execution after the Soviet Republic's overthrow, summed up the experience of working with Social Democrat and Independent Socialist 'allies': 'The Social-Democrats start, then run away and betray us. The Independents fall for the bait, join us, and then let us down. And we Communists are stood up against the wall. We Communists are all dead men on leave.'

The contagion spread further: to Spain, which experienced its *Trienio Bolchevista* ('Three Bolshevik Years') in 1918–20; to France, where the Socialist Party of 150,000 members voted to transform itself into a Communist Party affiliated to the Third International; and in Britain, where engineering

WORLD REVOLUTION? ◆ 221

workers fought pitched battles with police and soldiers on the streets of Glasgow in 1919, and the mining, transport, and rail unions formed a 'triple alliance' which terrified the Liberal government in 1920.

The revolutionary mood also infected distant continents: Australia, Canada, and the US experienced mass strikes as workers fought to build unions, raise wages, and improve conditions. It also passed from the major metropolitan countries to the colonial periphery. Irish Republicans waged guerrilla war to win independence in 1919–21. Huge Egyptian crowds demanded an end to British rule in 1919. Large parts of Iraq were in armed revolt against colonial occupation in 1920. Strikes, demonstrations, and riots swept British India in the post-war years. And Chinese students triggered a mass movement against foreign domination that would culminate in proletarian insurrection in 1927.

With hindsight we can see that 1921 was the turning point. The greatest popular revolt against war and poverty in the history of the world crashed against the defences of corporate capital and the imperialist states in a rising tide from 1917 to 1921. The system was shaken to its foundations and survived by a narrow margin. The revolutionary wave then ebbed back. Accidents of timing, failures of leadership, weakness of organisation, lack of unity, confusion of purpose: all contributed to the eventual defeat. The weave of interrelated narratives is too complex to be analysed here: it would be the subject of another book. But one thing is clear: at every turn, in every place, reformism, with its contradictory mix of social-democratic rhetoric and national-capitalist practice, acted to bamboozle and block the revolutionary movement of the working class; not once, not occasionally, but again and again whenever a decisive breakthrough seemed possible. This guaranteed the failure of the world revolution in 1917–21. And this doomed the Russian Revolution to isolation, and therefore to disintegration and defeat. This is the story that must now be told.

CHAPTER TEN

The Revolution Besieged

Defending the revolution. A Red Army recruitment
poster from the Civil War.

The Civil War

The Russian counter-revolution's first attempt to destroy the new Bolshevik regime had been easily and quickly suppressed. Strikes by public officials, sabotage by industrialists, and a sullen mood of non-cooperation among supporters of the old order failed to halt what Lenin called 'the triumphal march of soviet power'.[1] An attempted military coup by Kerensky and General Krasnov's Cossacks was defeated at the Battle of the Pulkovo Heights, a few miles south of Petrograd, on 30 October. Red artillery inflicted heavy losses (up to 500 dead), and the Cossacks, stunned by the resistance and demoralised by revolutionary agitation, retreated.[2]

The Constituent Assembly, which met on 5 January 1918, turned out to have an anti-Soviet majority. It comprised 370 Right SRs, 175 Bolsheviks, 86 Nationalists, 40 Left SRs, 17 Cadets, and 16 Mensheviks. This meant that the revolutionaries – the Bolsheviks and Left SRs – held only 30 per cent of the seats. A decision was taken to disperse the Constituent Assembly by force, eliminating a political centre that might otherwise have become a focus for counter-revolution. This was little more than a police action by the Soviet authorities in the capital: there were even fewer defenders of the Constituent Assembly than there had been of the Provisional Government.[3] But the political significance of the act was huge, and the controversy about it has raged for a century.

Since the earliest days of Russian socialism, all factions had called for such a body to lay the groundwork for a modern par-

---

1. Haynes 2002, 33.
2. Serge 1930/1972, 87–9.
3. Cliff 1978, 29–38.

liamentary democracy. The abrupt closure of the Constituent Assembly has been portrayed as a gross violation of democracy and a betrayal of past commitments. More than that: as a measure of the inherent authoritarianism of Lenin and the Bolsheviks. These arguments are flawed because they are abstract; only context can determine whether any particular act is progressive or reactionary. Up until February 1917, the call for a Constituent Assembly had been a revolutionary demand. Between February and October, it remained a slogan of radical forces seeking to push the revolution forwards to full democracy.

But the October Insurrection, the meeting of the Second Congress of Soviets, and the formation of the Council of People's Commissars had broken through the limits of formal representative democracy based on a parliament and created a mass participatory democracy based on Soviets. Formal democracy lags behind participatory democracy in giving expression to the will of the masses. Leaders elected in one phase of the revolution lag behind the radicalism of the masses in the next. Assemblies of the electoral majority lag behind the actions of the fighting vanguard. Revolution is above all a process of rapid change, in which nothing has time to coagulate, ossify, become fixed in form; its colossal transformative power repeatedly runs ahead of the consciousness of its protagonists. Men and women in revolutionary action frequently astonish themselves with their own audacity. Even Lenin, on the day of the insurrection, turned to Trotsky and said: 'You know, from persecution and life underground, to come so suddenly to power, it makes one giddy.' The Constituent Assembly was a relic from the past before it even met. 'This chief democratic slogan,' Trotsky explained, which had for a decade and a half tinged with its colour the heroic struggle of the masses, had grown pale and faded out, had somehow been ground between millstones, had become an empty shell, a form naked of content, a tradition and not a prospect. There was nothing mysterious in this process. The development of the revolution had reached the point of a direct battle for power between the two basic classes of society, the bourgeoisie and the proletariat. A Constituent Assembly could give nothing to either one or the other.[4]

Even so, despite the resilience of the Soviet regime, and the democracy and creativity that fizzed within it, backward, peasant-dominated, war-shattered, economically prostrate Russia was on borrowed time. Lenin was under no illusions. 'The final victory of socialism in a single country is ... impossible', he told the Third Soviet Congress in January 1918. 'Our contingent of workers and peasants which is upholding Soviet power is one of the contingents of the great world army.' Two months later he put the matter yet more starkly: 'It is the absolute truth that without a German revolution, we are doomed.'[5]

In the event, the German Revolution was first delayed by a year, then knocked back by a premature uprising, and finally aborted in a missed opportunity. In the meantime, with large parts of Soviet territory already under German occupation, and with Russian forces in no condition to resist a further advance, the Bolsheviks needed peace as a drowning man needs air. But the German generals were waging an imperialist war against a beaten enemy, and they refused to stop unless the

4.   Trotsky 1932–3/1977, 937–8.
5.   Faulkner 2013, 202.

Bolsheviks ceded Poland, Finland, the Baltic states, and large parts of the grain- and oil-rich Ukraine.

The German ultimatum split the Bolshevik leadership. Some argued for 'revolutionary war' in defence of Russian territory. Lenin argued for acceptance of the ultimatum, since the Bolsheviks had no forces with which to fight. Trotsky argued for neither revolutionary war nor acceptance of the ultimatum, trusting instead to the imminent outbreak of revolution in Germany. Trotsky's compromise position – neither war nor peace – was carried. But the German army on the Eastern Front simply rolled into the Ukraine, meeting virtually no resistance. Lenin then won the argument, and the Treaty of Brest-Litovsk was signed on 3 March 1918. The Soviet state was plundered of land, people, and resources – one-quarter of its territory, 45 per cent of its population, one-third of its agrarian output, 75 per cent of its coal and iron production, and almost 30 per cent of its revenues. That there was no alternative did not alter the bitterness of the recrimination nor the dire economic consequences. The daily bread ration in Petrograd had already fallen from 300gm in October 1917 to half that the following January, and to just 50gm in February – a tenth of a loaf. Now it got worse – and the revolution began to die slowly of starvation.[6]

Then civil war erupted in full fury. Instead of the comic-opera coup of a Kornilov or a Krasnov, this time it was a heavily armed, multi-front, years-long onslaught on the beleaguered enclave of workers' power around Petrograd and Moscow. The Whites – as the counter-revolutionaries were known – were mobilised on four main fronts under the command of former Tsarist generals: an eastern front under Kolchak in Siberia; a

---

6.   Cliff 1978, 38–54, esp. 50; Faulkner 2013, 202.

southern front under Kaledin, Denikin, and Wrangel in the Ukraine, the Don Basin, and the Caucasus; a western front under Yudenich in the Baltic region; and a distant northern front sustained by British, French, and US expeditionary forces based at Murmansk and Arkhangelsk.

Russia's great distances and primitive communications afforded the Whites ample opportunity to raise counter-revolutionary armies in distant quarters. Guns, funds, and additional fighting forces were provided by the foreign powers. Britain alone supplied nearly a million rifles. Some 14 foreign expeditionary forces invaded Russia in support of the Whites. Among the more significant interventions were a British operation around oil-rich Baku on the Caspian, a Japanese lodgement at Vladivostock on the Pacific, and the campaign of a Czech Legion recruited from former prisoners-of-war on the Trans-Siberian Railway. In the course of 1919, the workers' state was reduced to a central Russian zone of about 60 million people, largely cut off from its traditional sources of food, fuel, and raw materials.[7] The Russian Revolution, for a time, hung by a thread.

Yet by early 1920, most of the White armies had been defeated, and by the end of that year, the Civil War was effectively over. How was this possible? Because they were operating on exterior lines and widely separated fronts, the Whites were unable to co-ordinate their military operations. The Reds, on interior lines, were able to move forces quickly by rail to deal with successive emergencies in different sectors. Trotsky, despite his total lack of previous military experience, proved a brilliant leader of the Red Army, creating it from scratch from voluntary enlistment and then conscription. His

7.   Haynes 2002, 48; Faulkner 2013, 202.

method was to build it around a core of former Tsarist officers, Bolshevik commissars, and revolutionary workers and soldiers. This mix of professionalism and political commitment created a central military cadre able to organise and inspire the mass of mainly peasant recruits. By the end of 1918, there were 500,000 Red Army soldiers; by July 1919, the number was 2.3 million; and towards the end of the Civil War in July 1920, no less than 4 million.

The Red Army was far from perfect. It was sometimes poorly equipped, ill-disciplined, and badly led; it sometimes lacked the will to fight and failed in battle. It was, of necessity, held together by a ruthless military discipline; and often, to survive, like all armies in all ages, it was driven to forced requisitioning from civilians. Erich Wollenberg, a German Communist who fought with the Red Army in the Civil War, confessed the brutal reality:

As Trotsky most aptly remarked, the Bolsheviks were compelled to 'plunder all Russia' in order to satisfy the army's most basic needs. Trotsky certainly did not exaggerate, for in 1920 the army consumed 25% of the entire wheat production, 50% of other grain products, 60% of the fish and meat supplies, and 90% of all the men's boot and shoe wares ... The Bolsheviks were forced to commandeer all the peasants' surplus grain in order to ensure the supplies needed to feed the army and the industrial proletariat. The so-called 'requisition squads' and the system of forced quotas which extracted the peasants' last grain stores from their hiding-places and throttled all petty commerce were frequent causes of the peasantry's vacillation to the side of the Whites.[8]

8.   Wollenberg 1938/1978, 110–11.

Here was the contradiction destined to destroy the revolution. The 'plundering' enabled the Red Army to win the Civil War; but what remained of the Soviet state would be a shell. In the short term, the alternative seemed worse. The Whites represented the rule of the generals and the landlords; and the peasants knew that if they won, they would take back the land. And because they embodied the tyranny of the few over the many, the Whites were corrupt, brutal, and murderous. Captured commissars were routinely shot. Red soldiers perished in their thousands in White prisoner-of-war camps. Peasant villages were stripped of food and resources. Anti-Semitic pogroms killed up to 100,000 Jews. Even foreign officers sent to their aid were disgusted by the Whites. One American general reported that 'The Kolchak government has failed to command the confidence of anybody in Siberia except a small discredited group of reactionaries, monarchists, and former military officials.'[9] The Red Army, whatever its faults and failings, was a democratic army, a people's army, a would-be army of liberation. The White armies were the gangrenous limbs of a dying social order. That, in the end, ensured their defeat.

But the victory of the workers' state in the Russian Civil War was Pyrrhic. The effort had accelerated the economic collapse and drained the country of person-power, material resources, and revolutionary energy. The Tsarist counter-revolution had been defeated. But the revolution had been hollowed out. And, in one of history's most bitter twists, another species of counter-revolution – one without historic precedent – was already growing, a malignant embryo, inside the revolutionary regime itself.

9.   Cliff 1990, 58–87 passim; Haynes 2002, 49.

From War Communism to New Economic Policy

The Civil War accelerated the economic collapse and social transformation that were destroying the material and human foundations of the revolution. The towns were depopulated by lack of food and fuel, by unemployment as factories closed for lack of raw materials, and by mass recruitment of workers into the administration and the army. Grain requisitioning was introduced in the summer of 1918, to both feed the towns and supply the army, but this poisoned relations between the regime and the peasants. Centralised state control over the economy was imposed, but this was a desperate attempt to manage scarcity, and the black market boomed. By 1920, workers were receiving four-fifths of their wages in kind, and the value of these had fallen to one-tenth of their 1913 level. No-one could survive on this, so urban incomes were supplement by craft production, petty trade, and stealing; when this failed, people returned to the countryside, where most still had ties. Malnourished, often cold, dressed in filthy rags, the population was decimated by epidemic disease – typhus, typhoid, cholera, tuberculosis, and malaria. Russia probably suffered around 1.5 million excess civilian deaths between 1914 and 1917, but no less than 12 million between 1918 and 1922.

When the writer Ilya Ehrenburg arrived in Moscow, his trousers had disintegrated at the knees. With a new job, he was entitled to a clothing coupon. Getting to the front of the queue at a clothing depot, he was offered a choice: a winter coat or a suit. 'The choice was very hard. Frozen as I felt, I was ready to ask for a winter coat, but suddenly I remembered the humiliations of the past months and shouted, "Trousers! A suit." This rough-and-ready egalitarianism – an equalisation at the lowest level of existence – was called 'War Communism'. Some eternal optimists proclaimed it as the advent of socialism. Most understood it as desperation. 'What do you think?' asked one Bolshevik official. 'The People's Commissariat of Food does this for its own satisfaction? No. We do it because there is not enough food.'[10]

The Civil War and War Communism consumed the revolutionary cadre of 1917. The network of rank-and-file activists, eventually hundreds of thousands strong, that had led the masses during the October Insurrection was afterwards sucked into a huge apparatus of political administration and military defence. There was no choice. The landlords, capitalists, and bureaucrats of the old regime had fled. The estates, the factories, and the government departments were under new authority. An alternative workers' state had to be constructed to run the economy, manage society, and fight the counter-revolution, both in the rear and at the fronts.

Much of the work was repressive action, not just in battle against White armies, but in the towns and villages controlled by the Reds. Here was a bitter truth. Where there is abundance, there is enough for all. Where there is scarcity, there is a queue. Where there is a queue, you need a policeman. Just as you cannot build socialism in one country, nor can you build it on a foundation of poverty. Millstones of material deprivation were grinding into atoms the great mass forces mobilised in 1917, turning them to human dust, reducing the Russian *Narod* to a pitiful scrabble in the gutter for a crust of bread.

One measure of the shattered solidarity was the rise of the Cheka and the Red Terror. The Cheka was an internal

---

10. Haynes 2002, 51–4.

security police which grew to number 50,000 operatives during the Civil War. Its attempts to maintain order, suppress opposition, and root out counter-revolution seem to have claimed about 50,000 victims. Nor did its work end when the White armies were defeated. Red Russia was prostrate and riven with discontent. There were peasant revolts in Tambov province, strikes in Petrograd, and, most tragic of all, an armed insurrection at the naval base of Kronstadt, the great bastion of Bolshevism in 1917.[11]

The sailors raised no banner of counter-revolution; their slogan was 'Soviets without Communists'. The blame for everything – the ravages of the Civil War, the effects of Allied intervention and blockade, the privations of War Communism, the hunger, the cold, the disease, everything – was laid at the door of the embattled regime. It was a blind eruption of discontent lacking clear political purpose. But the rebels were adamant, and negotiations to find a peaceful settlement proved fruitless. Even Victor Serge, a deeply sensitive commentator, acutely aware of the germs of decay eating away at the revolution from within, believed the Bolsheviks had no choice but to crush the Kronstadt Rebellion of March 1921: 'They wanted to release a pacifying tempest, but all they could actually have done was open the way to counter-revolution ... Insurgent Kronstadt was not counter-revolution, but its victory would have led – without any shadow of a doubt – to the counter-revolution.' But he added something more: in the fighting at Kronstadt could be heard 'the crack of the timbers in the whole building'. Lenin thought so too. 'The Kronstadt

11.   Haynes 2002, 55–7.

events', he declared, 'were like a flash of lightning which threw more glare upon reality than anything else.'[12]

The great retreat now began. The Russian economy at the end of the Civil War in 1921 was only one fifth the size it had been in 1913. This was the economic cost of eight years of world war, revolution, and civil war in a vast country of primitive agriculture; not until 1928 would the 1913 level be regained. The world revolution that might have brought the wealth of German industry to the rescue of the besieged Soviet regime had stalled. The 'flash of lightning' at Kronstadt – like the thunderbolt of an angry Zeus – was clear warning that Russia's Bolsheviks had defeated the White armies only to find themselves confronting material barriers they could not surmount.

There were three insuperable problems: the social weight of the peasantry; the economic collapse due to war; and the disintegration of the working class. The alliance between workers and peasants had made the revolution possible. The peasants outnumbered the workers ten to one. If the workers had not won over the peasants, they would have been shot down by peasant-soldiers loyal to the Tsar. Instead, the Bolsheviks had promised 'bread, peace, and land', and the peasants had supported the October Insurrection; after that, even the plundering of the Red Army during the Civil War had not broken their deep-rooted class antagonism to the Whites.

But the interests of workers and peasants then diverged. The working class is a collective because its labour is collective. You cannot divide up a coal mine, an engineering plant, or a railway network into separate enterprises. When workers take power, they have to run the economy as an integrated whole.

12.   Cliff 1990, 184–6.

The peasantry, on the other hand, is a class of individualists, because every peasant's aspiration is to be an independent farmer. The peasants will support urban revolutionaries who allow them to seize the land. But further co-operation then depends on the ability of the towns to produce goods they can trade with the villages. If they fail in this, the peasants will not trade, and the towns will starve.

The Bolsheviks understood this. Their problem was that production had collapsed, the towns had emptied, and the working class had shrunk to a fraction of its former size, diminished by war, disease, retreat to the countryside, and absorption into the administration and army. In plain fact, the exploiting classes had been vanquished, the peasants controlled the land, the democratic mass movement in the cities had dissolved, and the only organised social force operating at a national level was the new bureaucratic apparatus of party and state.

Such was the economic and social malaise that had full Soviet democracy been restored in the early 1920s, the country would have been torn apart by the contradiction between the interests of the international working class and the interests of the Russian peasantry. The Bolsheviks were left holding onto power in the hope that they would eventually be rescued by world revolution. For a while, the socialist tradition itself could act as an historical force, even if embodied in a state apparatus rather than a revolutionary class. But the Bolsheviks could not defy gravity. Sooner or later, they would succumb to the hostile social forces all around them. Lenin could see it. 'Ours is not actually a workers' state', he said as early as 1920, 'but a workers' and peasants' state ... But that is not all. Our party programme shows that ours is a workers' state with bureaucratic distortions.' Later, alarmed at the influence of former Tsarist officials and newly recruited careerists in the government apparatus, he posed the question: 'This mass of bureaucrats – who is leading whom?'[13]

At the Tenth Party Congress in March 1921, War Communism was abandoned in favour of the New Economic Policy (NEP); it would remain the policy of the Soviet state until 1928. The NEP was an attempt to resolve the 'scissors crisis' between town and country, and thus to win an economic breathing-space before the next global revolutionary upsurge. It allowed private production and a free market to develop alongside state enterprise. The effect was to foster the development of a class of entrepreneurs (the 'NEP men') and a class of rich peasants (the *kulaks*). At the same time, the 'red industrialists' who ran state enterprises behaved increasingly like conventional capitalists. The imperatives of survival for an embattled state in control of an underdeveloped economy dominated by peasant farms were transforming the character of the regime.[14]

In 1928, Lenin's question – 'who is leading whom?' – would receive its definitive answer. Crushing both the Right (representing the NEP men and the *kulaks*) and the Left (representing the old revolutionary tradition), Stalin's Centre would emerge from the backrooms of the Bolshevik Party as the political expression of a new bureaucratic ruling class. The way in which that class was formed and took power, and the nature of the totalitarian regime and state-capitalist economy it created, is the subject of our final chapter.

---

13.   Faulkner 2013, 218–19.
14.   Haynes 2002, 57–9; Faulkner 2013, 219.

CHAPTER ELEVEN

Stalinism

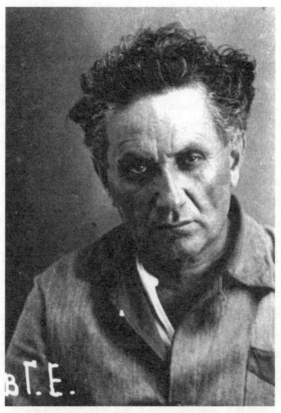

Crushing the revolution. Grigori Zinoviev, Lenin's
right-hand man, as photographed after his arrest by
Stalin's police in 1936 – one of millions of victims of the
counter-revolutionary terror.

The rise of the bureaucracy

By late 1921, almost everywhere in the world, the great revolutionary wave stirred into motion by the First World War was ebbing away. By late 1923, this was clear to all but the most die-hard optimists. Most critically, having faced down challenges from both Communist revolutionaries and Nazi counter-revolutionaries, Germany's Weimar Republic – a liberal parliamentary regime – had achieved a measure of stability. The October Insurrection of 1917 had not ignited the world socialist revolution that the Bolsheviks had worked for. Lenin himself became a poignant symbol of the decay of revolutionary hope: increasingly incapacitated by a series of strokes, he died in 1924. The Russian Revolution was left isolated, surrounded by enemies, devastated by war, and impoverished by economic collapse. Struggling to survive in desperate conditions, the Bolshevik regime turned in on itself and, in time, morphed into a hideous mockery of its former socialist ideals.

The crisis of 1918–21 – the period of the Civil War and War Communism – transformed the character of the Bolshevik Party, the Soviets, and the Russian working class. The close political relationship between revolutionary party, democratic assembly, and industrial proletariat had made possible the October Insurrection. Trotsky used the metaphor of a steam engine: the party was the piston, in which the energy of the revolution was transmitted; the democratic assemblies were the piston box, organising and concentrating the energy; and the industrial proletariat – along with the wider *Narod*, the soldiers and peasants, who followed its lead – were the steam, the mass collective action which powered all the great events of 1917. This relationship broke down completely in the subsequent four years with the disintegration of Russia's small industrial proletariat. 'The industrial proletariat is *déclassé*', Lenin declared in October 1921. 'It has ceased to exist as a proletariat. Since the great capitalist industry is ruined and the factories immobilised, the proletariat has disappeared.'[1] In the early 1920s, two main class forces dominated Russian life: the peasantry, now in control of the land, and the party-state bureaucracy, still infused with much revolutionary spirit, but increasingly preoccupied with the imperatives of restoring the basics of everyday life in a backward, war-ravaged, poverty-ridden economy.

The Bolshevik Party itself was transformed. Its membership swelled. The revolutionary veterans were soon swamped by post-October recruits, many joining because it was the only way to get a job and earn a living. By 1922, for example, only 15 per cent of Bolshevik Party members in Petrograd had been members in 1917; the proportion of 'Old Bolsheviks' – those who had been members *before* 1917 – was only a tiny fraction of the total.[2] The latter – now usually in leading positions – enjoyed great prestige. But this did little to foster inner-party democracy. Many of the new recruits were fair-weather friends of the regime, careerists rather than idealists, happy to go with the flow, unwilling to challenge the leadership. Nonetheless, the danger was that the political pressure of this mass of new party officials, the civil servants of the Soviet regime, would undermine the revolutionary traditions of the party. The adoption of the New Economic Policy and the rise of the NEP men and the *kulaks* increased this danger. The conservatism of

---

1. Haynes 2002, 64.
2. Haynes 2002, 53–5.

the new party bureaucracy might be reinforced by the social influence of this growing petty-bourgeois mass. They might also become transmitters into the party of the imperatives of world market competition, for the small Soviet economy, compelled to trade in order to survive, was being shaped by the international capitalist order. The Soviet state, Trotsky explained in 1927, was developing

> directly or indirectly, under the relative control of the world market. Herein lies the root of the question. The rate of development is not an arbitrary one – it is determined by the whole of world development, because in the last analysis world industry controls every one of its parts, even if that part is under the proletarian dictatorship and is building up socialist industry.[3]

Lenin spelt out the implications: 'The proletarian policy of the party is not determined by the character of the membership,' Lenin observed, 'but by the undivided prestige enjoyed by the small group that might be called the Old Guard of the party.' But in the growing social vacuum in which it operated, that 'Old Guard' felt compelled to shore up its defences: the Tenth Party Congress of March 1921 voted to ban internal factions – a major restriction on inner-party debate and democracy. This was one measure of the desperation with which the Bolshevik leadership acted to preserve the revolutionary tradition and maintain the Soviet regime as an outpost of socialist revolution pending the next global upsurge. But they were fighting a tragic battle against history. Beneath their feet was shifting sand. 'Permit me to congratulate you on being the vanguard

---

3. Haynes 2002, 60.

of a non-existent class' was the bitter reproach addressed to Lenin by one revolutionary veteran.[4]

At the end of his life, increasingly incapacitated by strokes, Lenin became preoccupied with the problem of bureaucratic degeneration. Sensing that his life's work was slipping away, he waged his 'last struggle' – against Joseph Stalin and the emerging party-state bureaucracy. In a secret 'Testament' written shortly before his death, he warned leading party comrades that the Secretary-General of the Party had 'unlimited authority concentrated in his hands', that he was 'too rude', and that they should therefore

> think about a way of removing Stalin from that post and appointing another man in his stead who in all other respects differs from Comrade Stalin in having only one advantage, namely, that of being more tolerant, more loyal, more polite, and more considerate to comrades, less capricious, etc.[5]

It was not to be. The party leadership felt too embattled on too many fronts to risk a split at the top. Lenin's prescription was, in any case, no remedy for the disease. Seeing no other way out, he had been reduced to proposing that the Bolshevik Revolution be rescued by a mere shuffling of its high command. The fundamental problem was not that Stalin was a boorish bureaucrat. It was that the political leadership of the emerging party-state apparatus required a boorish bureaucrat. The man whom Sukhanov remembered as 'a grey blur' in the great events of 1917 – a backroom operator, a party hack, not a mass leader, not an orator, writer, or theoretician – had now come

---

4.   Haynes 2002, 64–5.
5.   Cliff 1979, 201–16.

into his own. And as Secretary-General of the Party, in the new world coming into being – a bureaucratic dystopia more in keeping with a Kafka novel than a Marxist tract – he held the prime position, in control of appointments to every section of the party-state apparatus. Within a year of his taking up post, and even before Lenin's death, 10,000 new assignments had been made. The burgeoning bureaucracy – increasingly formed of men and women who owed their position to Stalin's faction – now dominated party congresses. More than half the delegates at the Twelfth Party Congress in April 1923 were party officials. A year later, at the Thirteenth Party Congress in May 1924, it was two-thirds. This was a critical turning point.

Not a single member of the internal party opposition was elected as a voting delegate to the Thirteenth Congress. Delegates were now chosen by processes of co-option and selection from above. Dissent and debate were minimal. Party democracy had been hollowed out. Nikolai Bukharin described how it worked in the Moscow party in late 1924:

> the secretaries of the party cells are usually appointed by the district committee … Normally the putting of the question to a vote takes place in a set pattern. They come and ask the meeting 'Who is against?', and since people more or less fear to speak out against, the individual in question finds himself elected secretary of the bureau of the cell … The same thing can be observed in a somewhat modified form in all other stages of the party hierarchy as well.[6]

The takeover by the party bureaucracy was given clear political expression by the adoption, at the Fourteenth Party

6. Haynes 2002, 67–8.

Congress in December 1925, of the doctrine of 'socialism in one country'. This amounted to the evisceration of the entire Marxist tradition – which can be defined as the theory and practice of international proletarian revolution – and of the Bolshevik tradition, which, true to Marxism, had insisted time and again that Russia was merely a link in a global chain, the 1917 revolution but a stage in a process, the Soviet regime dependent for its long-term survival on a new upsurge of revolutionary struggle on a worldwide scale.

But this perspective did not reflect the interests of the party-state bureaucracy. They were administrators involved in economic modernisation and social reconstruction; essentially, they were technocrats with a practical job of work to do. Increasingly, they were conscious of themselves as a group with common interests and shared goals; a group, indeed, that now formed the leadership of Soviet Russia. They were, according to Stalin, 'an order of Teutonic knights at the centre of the Soviet state'. More than that: as Christian Rakovsky and a group of Russian oppositionists observed in 1930, they were an embryonic ruling class:

> Before our very eyes, there has been and is being formed a large class of rulers with their own subdivisions, growing through controlled co-option ... What unites this peculiar sort of class is the peculiar sort of property, namely, state power ... [The bureaucracy] is the nucleus of a class ... Its appearance will mean that the working class will become another oppressed class. The bureaucracy is the nucleus of some kind of capitalist class, controlling the state and collectively owning the means of production.[7]

7. Haynes 2002, 68–9.

'Socialism in one country' (or 'national socialism') is a contradiction in terms. There is worldwide socialist revolution and there is the international capitalist system; there is no 'middle way', merely moments in a process of transition towards one or the other. Soviet Russia was metamorphosing into a form of what is best described as 'state-capitalism'. It was – as some oppositionists expressed it at the time of the Fourteenth Congress – becoming a 'radish': red on the outside, white on the inside. Between 1923/4 and 1928/9 – that is, between Lenin's death and the termination of the New Economic Policy – that process of transformation accelerated dramatically. The party expanded from half a million members to a million and a half. By the end of the decade, two-thirds of members had joined during the NEP years, most of them after Lenin's death. Lenin became a cult figure, his body mummified and put on display, his ideas turned into a catechism to be learned like religious dogma, with Stalin's dismal *Foundations of Leninism* as its missal.[8]

The destruction of opposition currents inside the party was easily accomplished. Though the highest levels of the state were convulsed by arguments around four critical issues – the growth of bureaucracy, the relations between town and country, the speed of economic development, and 'socialism in one country' versus international revolution – Stalin's Centre faction, resting on the support of the party-state apparatus it had itself created, remained predominant throughout. Successive oppositions were disoriented by an historical process they did not fully understand; but more importantly, they were disabled by their isolation inside the party machine,

8. Haynes 2002, 67–72.

while being unable – and to some degree unwilling – to build a political base outside it.

At first, Zinoviev and Kamenev formed a 'Troika' with Stalin against Trotsky's 'Left Opposition' (1922–5). Then, awakening to the danger represented by Stalin, they broke with him to form a 'United Opposition' in alliance with Trotsky (1925–7). Finally, with the United Opposition defeated, the alliance between Bukharin and Stalin disintegrated (1927–8), bringing the process of bureaucratic degeneration to its second great turning point – the moment when a new ruling class emerged fully fledged and took wing. 'Socialism in one country' now culminated in an all-out attempt to build a new state-capitalist economy based on the forced collectivisation of agriculture, intensified exploitation and capital accumulation, and state-driven investment in heavy industry and arms production. This, however, required the final destruction of what remained of Lenin's Bolshevik Party and the Russian revolutionary tradition.

The party-state bureaucracy that had emerged in Russia under Stalin's leadership was, by 1928, strong enough to complete what was, in effect, a counter-revolution. It had been accumulating power for a decade, and when it moved decisively at the end of the 1920s, it was able to destroy all remaining vestiges of working-class democracy. Meetings were packed, speakers shouted down, oppositionists purged and deported by an apparatus now dominated by officials who had joined it since the revolution.

During the 1930s, the bureaucracy consolidated its grip by liquidating virtually the whole of the old Bolshevik Party. Veterans of the October Insurrection were arrested, tortured, paraded in show trials, denounced as 'saboteurs' and 'wreckers', and then executed by Stalin's secret police. Against Trotsky and the tiny numbers of brave men and women who stood with him to the end was the power of inertia in an exhausted, impoverished, peasant country. Without world revolution to reinforce them, backward war-torn Russia had simply consumed its native revolutionaries – until they were so few that they could be swept into the oblivion of the Gulags.

Even so, the idealism and experience of the revolutionary years survived in popular memory and served to indict all that followed. For this reason, the remaining revolutionaries were hounded to their deaths during the 1930s. Only one in 14 of the Bolshevik Party's 1917 members still belonged to the Communist Party of the Soviet Union in 1939; virtually all of the rest were dead. Of the nine members of Lenin's last Politburo (in 1923), only two were still alive at the end of 1940 (Stalin and Molotov). Of the others, one died of natural causes (Lenin), one committed suicide in fear of arrest (Tomsky), and the remaining five were murdered (Kamenev, Zinoviev, Bukharin, Rykov, and Trotsky).

State-capitalism in Russia

The bureaucracy acted in 1928 because it had the power to do so and because it faced a crisis. The peasants were refusing to supply enough grain to the cities, and foreign governments were cutting off diplomatic relations and banning trade links. There was growing fear of war. The Russian state was no longer the centre of world revolution it had been in 1921. It was again, as it had been under the Tsars, one of Europe's great powers. Its defence was no longer seen to be a matter of proclamations and proletarian solidarity, but of tanks and heavy artillery. The leadership's response to the crisis of 1928/9 was to seize the grain, drive down wages, and impose rapid industrialisation. The Russian dictator explained the logic: 'To slacken the pace of industrialisation would mean to lag behind, and those who lag behind are beaten … We are 50 to 100 years behind the advanced countries. We must make good this lag in ten years or they will crush us.'[9]

Russia had survived civil war and foreign invasion: the new regime had not been destroyed by military force. But the defeat of the world revolution had left Russia isolated and impoverished in a global economy dominated by capitalism. So the counter-revolution was achieved not by violent overthrow, but by the relentless external pressure of economic and military competition. Russia needed to export grain to pay for machine tools. It needed machine tools to build modern industries. It needed these to produce the guns, tanks, and planes with which to defend itself in a predatory global system of competing nation-states. Private capital accumulation was too slow. What Bukharin in the 1920s had called 'socialism at a snail's pace' would have left Russia trailing behind and ever vulnerable to dismemberment by hostile powers. Only the state had the power to concentrate resources, impose a plan, override opposition, and drive through rapid forced industri- alisation. The aim was mass production to build state power. Russia's rulers thus became personifications of state-capitalist accumulation. But they also used their power to reward themselves richly, even as they plundered the peasantry, cut wages, increased work pressure, and filled the Gulags with slave-labourers.

9.   Faulkner 2013, 231.

By 1937, plant directors were paid 2,000 roubles a month, skilled workers 200–300 roubles, and workers on the minimum wage 110–115 roubles. Pay differentials in the army were even more extreme: during the Second World War, colonels were paid 2,400 roubles a month, private soldiers 10. The pay of plant directors and army colonels was modest, however, compared with that of top members of the state bourgeoisie earning up to 25,000 roubles a month – more than 200 times the minimum wage. So the bureaucracy had become a privileged class with a clear material interest in remaining loyal to Stalin and the state-capitalist system. It therefore proved utterly ruthless in imposing forced industrialisation on society at a colossal cost in human suffering.

Consumption was sacrificed to investment in heavy industry. The proportion of investment devoted to plant, machinery, and raw materials – as opposed to consumer goods – rose from 33 per cent in 1927/8 to 53 per cent by 1932 and 69 per cent by 1950. The result was shortages and queues – though less than there might have been, because wages were cut at the same time, by an estimated 50 per cent over six years. Grain was seized from the peasantry to feed the growing urban population and to pay for imports of foreign machinery. Because of this, when the price collapsed on world markets in 1929, at least three million peasants starved to death. It was not enough. The state decreed 'the collectivisation of agriculture' (state control). Millions of peasants – denounced as *kulaks* (rich peasants producing for the market) – were dispossessed and transported. Many died. Others ended up as slave-labourers in the Gulags, which expanded into a vast Siberian slave empire run by Stalin's security apparatus. The 30,000 prisoners of 1928 had become two million by 1931, five million by 1935, and probably more than ten million by the end of the decade. Millions of others were simply murdered by the police, the annual cull rising from 20,000 in 1930 to 350,000 in 1937. State terror on this scale reflected Russian backwardness, the pace of state-capitalist accumulation, and the levels of exploitation necessary to achieve it. The working class, the peasantry, and the national minorities had to be pulverised into submission.[10]

The damage was not confined to Russia. The revolutionary content of Marxism was abandoned but its verbal formulas were retained and redeployed to justify the policies of the Russian bureaucracy. The Comintern – the Communist International – became a vehicle for imposing the ideology and policies of the Russian state on foreign Communist parties. In 1927, having abandoned world revolution in favour of 'socialism in one country', Stalin tried to break out of Russia's isolation by seeking respectable allies abroad. So the Chinese Communist Party was ordered to kow-tow to Chiang Kai-shek and disarm the Shanghai working class. The result was a terrible counter-revolutionary massacre. The following year, the policy suddenly switched to sectarianism and adventurism. In the Comintern's disastrous 'Third Period', Stalin proclaimed a new revolutionary advance, such that Communists were to break all ties with Social Democrats and prepare for an imminent seizure of power.

This mirrored (and helped justify) the policy inside Russia. The attack on the *kulaks* was presented as an attack on private capitalism (which was true) and as a major advance towards 'socialism' (which was not). The ultra-left turn of the Third Period provided a smokescreen for bureaucratic power and

---

10. Faulkner 2013, 229–32; the classic study of this process is Tony Cliff's State Capitalism in Russia, one of the seminal works of modern Marxist analysis.

forced industrialisation. The sectarianism of the Third Period created a fatal division inside the German labour movement and allowed Hitler to take power in 1933.

But the Nazis threatened a resurgence of aggressive German imperialism, and Stalin began casting around for European allies. The Comintern therefore lurched from ultra-left madness to 'Popular Frontism': Communists were now to form alliances with the liberal bourgeoisie, reining back the working class to placate potential allies of the Russian state.

Thus, instead of promoting world revolution, the Stalinist Comintern had, by the mid 1930s, become actively counter-revolutionary. This was to produce, in 1937, another catastrophic disaster to place alongside those of 1927 and 1933, when the Spanish Communist Party, under orders from Moscow, spearheaded the suppression of the working-class revolt in Catalonia, decapitating the entire revolutionary movement inside the Spanish Republic and derailing the struggle against Franco's fascists. The Spanish workers would pay a terrible price: 40 years of right-wing dictatorship.

With the triumph of Stalin in Russia in 1928 and of Hitler in Germany in 1933 a terrible darkness descended on Europe. The continent became a place of dictatorship, persecution, and militarism. Later it would explode into war – the most terrible war in history, one in which 60 million would die, most of them in mass campaigns of genocide and ethnic-cleansing. The horrors of Stalingrad, Auschwitz, and the Gulags were the bitter fruit of revolutionary defeat, counter-revolutionary triumph, and a world gone mad. They were the historic confirmation of the chilling prediction made long before by the German-Polish revolutionary Rosa Luxemburg that humanity faced a choice between socialism and barbarism. We face it still.

EPILOGUE

A Century of War and Revolution

The century since 1917 has been a century of war and revolution. The political crisis unleashed by the Russian Revolution was global and protracted. Even after the main storm had passed, Germany was again on the brink of revolution in 1923, Britain experienced the General Strike in 1926, and China was convulsed by revolution and counter-revolution in 1927.

After the Wall Street Crash of 1929, unemployment and poverty skyrocketed, and politics polarised across Europe. The Nazis took power in Germany in 1933, but the workers of Vienna, Paris, and Barcelona waged mighty struggles to halt the fascist advance between 1934 and 1938.

The Second World War conjured insurrectionary movements in Yugoslavia, Warsaw, Greece, Italy, and many other places. Under the shadow of the Bomb, the Cold War era saw nationalist movements in China, Cuba, Algeria, Vietnam, and a dozen other countries wage guerrilla insurgencies to overthrow colonial rule. In 1956, Arab nationalists faced down European imperialism in the Suez crisis, and Hungarian workers fought Russian tanks on the streets of Budapest.

Between 1968 and 1975, the world was again convulsed by upheavals on a scale reminiscent of the great revolutionary wave of 1917 to 1923. In May-June 1968, French students fought pitched battles with riot police in Paris, while millions of workers went on strike and occupied their factories. Across the world, millions were mobilised in mass struggles against war, racism, exploitation, and police violence. In 1974, military dictatorships were overthrown in Greece and Portugal.

We live still in an epoch of war and revolution. Mass urban insurrection brought down a US-backed dictator in Iran in 1979. A revolutionary trade-union movement paralysed Poland in 1981. The Stalinist regimes of Russia and Eastern Europe were swept away by a chain-reaction of popular uprisings in 1989. Middle Eastern dictators were toppled or destabilised in the 'Arab Spring' of 2010–12. In the last few years, we have been witness to a string of popular uprisings that have turned some of the urban heartlands of world capitalism – Athens, Madrid, Istanbul, Rio, and many more – into battlegrounds.

These waves of popular resistance have crashed against bastions of corporate and state power and each time receded. What they confirm is that the rich and the warlords – the corporate and politico-military elites who control our lives – live at permanent risk of revolt from below. And they know – because, as the English revolutionary poet Percy Bysshe Shelley put it, 'they are few and we are many' – that such revolt could, at some point, acquire the mass, energy, and direction to sweep them and their rotten system away.

That this happens – that we make a worldwide anti-capitalist revolution – has now become an existential imperative. The global economy is trapped in a long-term crisis of stagnation-slump, hooked on debt, speculation, and bubbles of electronic money. Whole societies have imploded into sectarian warfare and mass displacement. Other societies are being torn apart by soaring inequality and deprivation. The greed of the rich, the profiteering of the corporations, the violence of imperial states, the carbon pollution of the global growth-machine, the privatisation of public services, the grinding down of the poor, the militarisation of the refugee crisis, the shoot-to-kill racism of police, the bigotry and hate pumped out by right-wing politicians and broadcast by the mass media, all this and much more reveals a deeply dysfunctional, pathological, redundant social order.

As I wrote at the end of the *Marxist History of the World*:

A different world has become an absolute historical necessity. Another world is possible. The revolution is, in this sense, an 'actuality'. But it is not a certainty. It has to be fought for. Its achievement depends on what we all do. The historical stakes have never been higher.

The Russian Revolution of 1917 is rich in lessons for today's crisis-ridden world of exploitation, oppression, and violence. The Bolsheviks have much to teach us.

Timeline

Date	Events in Russian history	Events in the wider world
1462–1505	Reign of Tsar Ivan the Great	
1533–1584	Reign of Tsar Ivan the Terrible	
1570	Destruction of Novgorod	
1598–1613	'Time of Troubles'	
1613	Accession of Tsar Michael Romanov	
1670–1671	Rural revolt of Razin	
1682–1725	Reign of Tsar Peter the Great	
1700–1721	Great Northern War	
1707–1708	Rural revolt of Bulavin	
1762–1796	Reign of Tsarina Catherine the Great	
1773–1775	Rural revolt of Pugachev	
1792–1815		French Revolutionary and Napoleonic Wars
1812	Napoleon's failed invasion of Russia	
1825 14 December	Decembrist Revolt in St Petersburg	
1848		Year of Revolutions/ 'Springtime of Peoples'
1853–1856	Crimean War	
1857	First publication of radical journal *The Bell* (by Herzen, in London)	
1861	Abolition of serfdom	
1863	Publication of Chernyshevsky's *What is to be Done?*	

Date	Events in Russian history	Events in the wider world
1869	Publication of Tolstoy's *War and Peace*	
1874–1875	Narodniks 'go to the people'	
1876 6 December	'Land and Liberty' demonstration in St Petersburg	
1877–1878	Russo-Turkish War	
1881 13 March	Assassination of Tsar Alexander II by *Narodnya Volya* revolutionaries	
1883	Plekhanov founds Emancipation of Labour Group	
1891–1903	Government dominated by reforming minister Sergei Witte	
1894	Accession of Tsar Nicholas II	
1894–1895		First Sino-Japanese War
1895	Lenin and others found St Petersburg League of Struggle for Emancipation of the Working Class	
1898	'First Congress' of Russian Social Democratic Labour Party (RSDLP) in Minsk	
1900 December	First publication of revolutionary newspaper *Iskra* (by Lenin, in Leipzig)	
1902	Lenin publishes *What is to be Done?*	
1903 July–August	Second Congress of RSDLP in Brussels and London	
1904–1905	Russo-Japanese War	
1905		
9 January	'Bloody Sunday': 1905 Revolution begins	

Date	Events in Russian history	Events in the wider world
April–May	Third ('Bolshevik') Congress of RSDLP in London	
27 May	Battle of Tsushima: Russian naval defeat	
10–21 October	General strike	
13 October	Formation of St Petersburg Soviet	
22–24 November	General strike	
3 December	Suppression of St Petersburg Soviet	
9–17 December	Armed insurrection in Moscow	
1906		
April–May	Fourth ('Unity') Congress of RSDLP in Stockholm	
April–July	First Tsarist Duma	
1906–1911	Government dominated by reforming minister Peter Stolypin	
1907		
February–June	Second Tsarist Duma	
April–May	Fifth Congress of RSDLP in London	
November 1907–June 1912	Third Tsarist Duma	
1912		
January	Sixth ('Bolshevik') Congress of RSDLP in Prague	

Date	Events in Russian history	Events in the wider world
4 April	Massacre of striking workers in Lena goldfields, Siberia	
April 1912–July 1914	Wave of mass strikes across Russia	
November 1912– October 1917	Fourth Tsarist Duma	
1914		
28 June		Assassination of Archduke Franz Ferdinand in Sarajevo
July	Three-week general strike by 300,000 St Petersburg workers	
28 July		100,000 German workers demonstrate against war in Berlin
4 August		German SPD votes to support war in Reichstag
August	Battle of Tannenburg: Russian defeat	
September	Battle of the Masurian Lakes: Russian defeat	
November	Arrest of Bolshevik Duma fraction	
1915		
February	Battle of Augustowo: Russian defeat	
April– September	Strike wave involves 400,000 workers	
May–June	Battle of Gorlice-Tarnow: Russian defeat	

Date	Events in Russian history	Events in the wider world
1916		
January–June	Lenin writes *Imperialism: The Highest Stage of Capitalism*	
June–September	Brusilov Offensive: Russian victory at heavy cost	
15/16 December	Assassination of Rasputin	
1917		
9 January	150,000 workers demonstrate in Petrograd on anniversary of Bloody Sunday	
23 February	90,000 workers strike in Petrograd: the beginning of 'February Days' revolution	
24 February	180,000 workers strike in Petrograd and clash with police	
25 February	240,000 workers strike in Petrograd and defeat police	
26 February	Soldiers deployed against workers in Petrograd	
27 February	Petrograd military garrison mutinies and joins revolution – 400,000 workers on strike, 150,000 soldiers in mutiny; strikes and demonstrations begin in Moscow	
1 March	Executive Committee of Petrograd Soviet concedes power to First Provisional Government; Petrograd Soviet passes Order No 1	
3 April	Lenin arrives from exile at Petrograd's Finland Station	

Date	Events in Russian history	Events in the wider world
4 April	Lenin issues *April Theses* calling for overthrow of Provisional Government	
20–21 April	Mass anti-war demonstrations in Petrograd: 'April Days'	
22 April	Second Provisional (Coalition) Government formed	
24–29 April	Seventh ('Bolshevik') Congress of the RSDLP in Petrograd	
May-June	First Conference of Petrograd Factory Committees (Bolshevik dominated)	French Army mutinies on Western Front
June	First All-Russian Congress of Soviets in Petrograd	
18 June	400,000 join Bolshevik-dominated Soviet demonstration in Petrograd	
1–19 July	Kerensky Offensive: Russian defeat	
3–4 July	500,000 join armed, semi-insurrectionary, Bolshevik-dominated demonstrations in Petrograd: 'July Days'	
19 July	Bolshevik leaders arrested or forced into hiding	
24 July	Third Provisional (Coalition) Government formed	
7–12 August	Second Conference of Petrograd Factory Committees	
12 August	State Conference opens in Moscow; 400,000 workers mount protest strike	
14 August	Kornilov addresses State Conference	
21 August	Fall of Riga to Germans	

Date	Events in Russian history	Events in the wider world
22–27 August	Kornilov's attempted coup	
1 September	Petrograd Soviet votes for government of workers and peasants	
10 October	Bolshevik Central Committee (meeting in secret) votes for armed insurrection	
13 October	Soldiers' Section of Petrograd Soviet votes to obey only Military Revolutionary Committee orders	
17–22 October	All-Russian Conference of Factory Committees in Petrograd	
18 October	Petrograd Garrison Conference votes for armed insurrection	
20 October	Trotsky elected Chair of the Military Revolutionary Committee	
21 October	Petrograd Garrison Conference votes to obey only Military Revolutionary Committee orders	
22 October	'Peaceful review of forces' in Petrograd: hundreds of thousands attend mass meetings to endorse Soviet power	
24 October	Provisional Government attempts to suppress insurrectionary movement	
25 October	Military Revolutionary Committee completes takeover of Petrograd	
26 October	Fall of Winter Palace and arrest of Provisional Government	
25–27 October	Second All-Russian Congress of Soviets in Petrograd	
October-November		Battle of Caporetto: Italian defeat and rout

Date	Events in Russian history	Events in the wider world
1918		
5–6 January	Constituent Assembly dissolved by Soviet authorities	
3 March	Treaty of Brest-Litovsk signed	
29 October		German naval mutiny triggers German Revolution
9 November		Revolution in Berlin
11 November		Armistice on Western Front
February 1918– November 1920	Russian Civil War (period of intensive fighting)	
1919		
4–15 January		Spartakus Rising in Berlin: revolutionaries defeated and Liebknecht and Luxemburg murdered
21 January		Start of Irish War of Independence
31 January		'Battle of George Square': street battle between striking workers and police in Glasgow
March	First Congress of Third International	
March–July		Egyptian anti-colonial revolt

Date	Events in Russian history	Events in the wider world
March–August		Hungarian Soviet Republic under Bela Kun
April–May		Bavarian Soviet Republic
4 May		Start of Chinese Revolution
1919–1920		*Biennio Rosso* ('Two Red Years') in Italy
1920		
13 March		Kapp Putsch in Germany: defeated by working-class uprising
May–October		Iraqi anti-colonial revolt
July–August	Second Congress of Third International	
August 1920		General strike and factory occupations by 500,000 workers in Italy's northern 'industrial triangle'
1921		
March	Kronstadt Rebellion; Tenth Party Congress: 'War Communism' abandoned, 'New Economic Policy' adopted, internal factions banned	
June–July	Third Congress of Third International	

Date	Events in Russian history	Events in the wider world
1922		
October		Mussolini's 'March on Rome': Fascist seizure of power in Italy
November–December	Fourth Congress of Third International	
1922–1925	Trotsky's 'Left Opposition' active	
1923		
March	Lenin suffers third stroke and is incapacitated	
April	Twelfth Party Congress	
1924		
21 January	Death of Lenin	
May	Thirteenth Party Congress	
December 1925	Fourteenth Party Congress: adoption of policy of 'socialism in one country'	
1925–1927	Trotsky and Zinoviev's 'United Opposition' active	
April 1927		Shanghai Massacre of Chinese Communists
1927–1928	Alliance between Stalin and Bukharin disintegrates	
1928–1933		'Third Period' ultra-left strategy and tactics imposed on foreign Communist parties
January 1933		Hitler takes power in Germany

Date	Events in Russian history	Events in the wider world
1933–1939		'Popular Front' alliances imposed on foreign Communist parties
1936–1938	Moscow show trials and execution of Old Bolshevik leaders	
May 1937		Stalinist counter-revolution destroys workers' movement in Barcelona, Spain

Bibliography

I have restricted the bibliography to works cited in the notes. I should alert readers to the fact that I have drawn heavily in places on my own *Marxist History of the World*. Apologies to the occasional reader who may find themselves treading some of the same ground, but, as the saying goes, 'if it ain't broke, don't fix it'.

Badayev, A. Y., 1929/1987, *Bolsheviks in the Tsarist Duma*, London, Bookmarks.

Chamberlin, W. H., 1935/1965, *The Russian Revolution: Volume I, 1917–1918, From the Overthrow of the Tsar to the Assumption of Power by the Bolsheviks*, New York, Universal Library.

Chernyshevsky, N. G., 1863/1961, *What is to be Done?*, New York, Vintage Books.

Cliff, T., 1955/1974, *State Capitalism in Russia*, London, Pluto.

Cliff, T., 1959/1983, *Rosa Luxemburg*, London, Bookmarks.

Cliff, T., 1975/1986, *Lenin, Vol. 1: Building the Party, 1893–1914*, London, Bookmarks.

Cliff, T., 1976, *Lenin, Vol. 2: All Power to the Soviets*, London, Pluto.

Cliff, T., 1978, *Lenin, Vol. 3: Revolution Besieged*, London, Pluto.

Cliff, T., 1979, *Lenin, Vol. 4: The Bolsheviks and World Revolution*, London, Pluto.

Cliff, T., 1987, 'Introduction', in A. Y. Badayev, *Bolsheviks in the Tsarist Duma*, London, Bookmarks.

Cliff, T., 1989, *Trotsky: Towards October, 1879–1917*, London, Bookmarks.

Cliff, T., 1990, *Trotsky: The Sword of the Revolution, 1917–1923*, London, Bookmarks.

Connaughton, R., 2003, *Rising Sun and Tumbling Bear*, London, Cassell.

Draper, H., 1978, *Karl Marx's Theory of Revolution: Volume II, The Politics of Social Classes*, New York, Monthly Review Press.

Dupuy, R. E. and Dupuy, T. N., 1970, *The Encyclopedia of Military History, from 3500 BC to the Present*, London, Macdonald & Jane's.

Engels, F., 1848/1973, 'Speeches on Poland (22 February 1848)', in K. Marx, *The Revolutions of 1848: Political Writings, Vol. 1*, ed. D. Fernbach, Harmondsworth and London, Penguin/New Left Review.

Farrell, A., 1992, *Crime, Class, and Corruption: The Politics of the Police*, London, Bookmarks.

Faulkner, N., 2013, *A Marxist History of the World: From Neanderthals to Neoliberals*, London, Pluto.

Faulkner, N., 2014, 'The Age of Neoliberal Austerity, Part 4, Revolutionary Organisation', at http://neilfaulknersblog.blogspot.co.uk

Fitzpatrick, S., 1982/1984, *The Russian Revolution, 1917–1932*, Oxford, Oxford University Press.

Glatter, P., 2005, *The Russian Revolution of 1905: Change Through Struggle*, London, Porcupine.

Goodlad, G., 2015, 'For God and Tsar: Imperial Russia's Army from the Crimea to World War I', *Military History Monthly*, 63, 18–24.

Haynes, M., 2002, *Russia: Class and Power, 1917–2000*, London, Bookmarks.

Kochan, L., 1967/1970, *Russia in Revolution*, London, Paladin.

Kochan, L. and Abraham, R., 1962/1990, *The Making of Modern Russia*, London, Penguin.

Krupskaya, N. K., 1960/1975, *Reminiscences of Lenin*, New York, International Publishers.

Le Blanc, P., 1993/2015, *Lenin and the Revolutionary Party*, Chicago, Haymarket.

Lenin, V. I., 1898, *The Development of Capitalism in Russia*, in *Selected Works*, London: Lawrence & Wishart, 1, 219–385.

Lenin, V. I., 1901, *Where to Begin?*, in *Collected Works*, London: Martin Lawrence, 4, 1, 109–16.

Lenin, V. I., 1902, *What is to be Done?*, in *Selected Works*, 2, 25–192.

Lenin, V. I., 1908, *The Agrarian Question in Russia at the End of the 19th Century*, in *Selected Works*, 1, 137–217.

Lenin, V. I., 1917a, *Letters from Afar*, in *Selected Works*, 6, 3–12.

Lenin, V. I., 1917b, *Tasks of the Proletariat in the Present Revolution*, in *Selected Works*, 6, 21–6.

Lenin, V. I., 1917c, *A Dual Power*, in *Selected Works*, 6, 27–30.

Lenin, V. I., 1917d, *The Second All-Russian Congress of Soviets of Workers' and Soldiers' Deputies: To the Workers, Soldiers, and Peasants*, in *Selected Works*, 6, 399–400.

Lih, L. T., 2008/2013, *Lenin Rediscovered: What is to be Done? in Context*, Delhi, Historical Materialism/Aakar Books.

Lih, L. T., 2011, *Lenin*, London, Reaktion Books.

Lincoln, W. B., 1986, *Passage Through Armageddon: The Russians in War and Revolution, 1914–1918*, New York, Simon & Schuster.

Lukács, G., 1924/1970/2009, *Lenin: A Study on the Unity of his Thought*, London, Verso.

Marx, K., 1852/1869/1973, *The Eighteenth Brumaire of Louis Bonaparte*, in *Surveys from Exile*, Harmondsworth and London, Penguin/New Left Review, 143–249.

Nettl, P., 1966/1969, *Rosa Luxemburg*, London, Oxford University Press.

Piatnitsky, O., 1935, *Memoirs of a Bolshevik*, London, Martin Lawrence.

Pipes, R., 1974/1977, *Russia Under the Old Regime*, Harmondsworth, Penguin.

Plekhanov, G., 1904/1978, 'Programme of the RSDLP', in *1903: Second Congress of the Russian Social Democratic Labour Party*, trans. B. Pearce, London, New Park.

Ransome, A., 1919/1992, *Six Weeks in Russia, 1919*, London, Redwords.

Ransome, A., 1976, *The Autobiography of Arthur Ransome*, London, Jonathan Cape.

Raskolnikov, F. F., 1925/1982, *Kronstadt and Petrograd in 1917*, London, New Park.

Reed, J., 1926/1977, *Ten Days That Shook the World*, Harmondsworth, Penguin.

RSDLP, 1904/1978, *1903: Second Congress of the Russian Social Democratic Labour Party*, trans. B. Pearce, London, New Park.

Salisbury, H. E., 1977/1978, *Black Night, White Snow: Russia's Revolutions, 1905–1917*, London, Cassell.

Sender, T., 1940, *The Autobiography of a German Rebel*, London, Labour Book Service.

Serge, V., 1930/1972, *Year One of the Revolution*, trans. P. Sedgwick, London, Allen Lane.

Shlyapnikov, A., 1923/1982, *On the Eve of 1917*, London, Allison & Busby.

Smith, S. A., 1983, *Red Petrograd: Revolution in the Factories, 1917–18*, Cambridge, Cambridge University Press.

Steinberg, M. D. (ed.), 2001, *Voices of Revolution, 1917*, New Haven and London, Yale University Press.

Stevenson, D., 2004, *1914–1918: The History of the First World War*, London, Allen Lane.

Stone, N., 1969/1971, 'The Kerensky Offensive', in *Purnell's History of the First World War*, London: Purnell, Vol. 6, 2448–53.

Strachan, H., 2001/2003, *The First World War, Vol. I: To Arms*, Oxford, Oxford University Press.

Sukhanov, N. N., 1955/1984, *The Russian Revolution, 1917: A Personal Record*, Princeton, Princeton University Press.

Trotsky, L., 1932–3/1977, *The History of the Russian Revolution*, London, Pluto.

Trotsky, L., 1971/1975, *My Life: An Attempt at an Autobiography*, Harmondsworth, Penguin.

Wollenberg, E., 1938/1978, *The Red Army*, London, New Park.

Zinoviev, G., 1923/1973, *History of the Bolshevik Party, from the Beginnings to February 1917*, London, New Park.

Index